JUDY MARTIN

THE BLOCK BOOK

CROSLEY-GRIFFITH PUBLISHING COMPANY, INC.

Grinnell, Iowa

━━ IMPORTANT COPYRIGHT INFORMATION ━━

ISBN 0-929589-05-X
Published by Crosley-Griffith Publishing Company, Inc.
P.O. Box 512, Grinnell, Iowa 50112
(515) 236-4854 phone or fax
e-mail crosgriff@aol.com

Photography by O'Connor Photography, Grinnell, Iowa
and Robert Willits Photography, Des Moines, Iowa
Printed in U.S.A. by Quebecor Printing, Dubuque, Iowa

First Printing 1998
15 14 13 12 11 10 9 8 7 6 5 4 3 2 1

CONTENTS

COLOR PHOTOGRAPHS

ACKNOWLEDGMENTS

Many thanks to Steve Bennett, Jean Nolte, and Chris Hulin for their tireless proofreading and suggestions and to Phil Moore for inputting some of the computer art.

Special thanks to Chris Hulin, Margy Sieck, Diane Tomlinson, Jane Bazyn, and Jean Nolte for making blocks beyond the call of duty. Thanks also to the many friends who made one or two blocks: Viola Armstrong, Genevieve Bailey, Dawn Bowman, Patsy Carr, Donna Davis, Mary Hazelwood, Sharon Jolly, Rebecca Loew, Linda Medhus, Dorothy Palmer, Lois Rhinehart, Aileen Taylor, Janet Westberg, and Ardis Winters.

Thanks to all the visitors to our website, http://quilt.com/judym, who entered the Name the Block Contest. Sincere thanks to Sue Traudt at the World Wide Quilting Page for making the contest possible. Finally, thanks to contest winners, Joan Lush, who suggested the name "Cyberstar," Lori King, for "Night & Day Variation," and Kellie Page, for "Sailing by the Stars."

Blocks are the mainstay of quiltmaking. They are the basic design unit as well as the main construction unit for most quilts. Blocks have fascinated quilters for generations. They certainly have captured my imagination! This is my third book on the subject.

When I wrote my first block book in 1988, I called it *Judy Martin's Ultimate Book of Quilt Block Patterns.* I called it "ultimate," because it far exceeded the 1988 norm for block pattern books, being the first to sport color photographs. Now, ten years later, *The Block Book* sets a new standard. Bigger color photos, shaded drawings, an easy-to-use format, and rotary cutting directions are among the improvements. The blocks, themselves, are the biggest improvement.

Blocks for a New Generation in Today's Fabrics

The block designs are mostly new ones in a traditional vein. Today's exciting fabrics, from batiks and hand-dyed fabrics to antique reproductions, make the blocks sing! Some of the block designs lend themselves to contemporary looks with their eccentric arrangement of elements. I designed a number of blocks with small, off-center stars superimposed over bigger stars. Look for these throughout the book. The sewing is often a cinch, although the blocks appear complex and enigmatic.

Blocks Sized for Precision

Blocks are arranged by size, with nearly half being the popular 12" finished size. Except in the typical sampler quilt, blocks don't have to be any particular size, so I didn't hesitate to make a third of the blocks in a 10¼" size. This may sound odd, but it is the perfect size for blocks based on the proportions of a LeMoyne Star rather than a grid of squares. These are among the most elegant of blocks and easily my favorites. A 10¼" rotary-cut LeMoyne Star is an amazing 50 times more accurate than a 12" rotary-cut LeMoyne Star! There are enough 10¼" and 12" blocks here to make a sampler quilt in either block size. Smaller blocks and great big ones complete *The Block Book.*

Grand Blocks: Quilts All By Themselves

With wall quilts continuing to grow in popularity, I wanted to include blocks that would be spectacular enough to be quilts all by themselves. I call these big, impressive blocks "Grand Blocks." Grand blocks also make terrific medallion centers, worthy of all the hoopla of myriad pieced borders. Grand Blocks can also be used as building blocks for quilts, with only a few blocks needed for a bed-sized quilt.

Blocks: The Building Blocks for Quilts

Quilt blocks are the basic building blocks of most quilts. Turning blocks into quilts is often a simple matter of joining blocks side by side. Sometimes a border is added, and sometimes sashes or alternate plain blocks separate the individual blocks. So, you see, this book is more than just a collection of block patterns. It is also a pattern book for all kinds of quilts that are just waiting to be made.

Collecting Blocks

As the main part of the quilt pattern, blocks were traditionally collected to record quilt patterns for future use. A block collection can also record quilts that you have made and parted with. How I wish that I had such a record of my first quilts made in the late '60s and early '70s! Imagine how quaint those fabrics would look today.

Block Samplers

When we think of quilt blocks, most of us think of sampler quilts made of a variety of blocks. Often, these are set simply with sashes. In this book you will find instructions for a terrific new look for sampler quilts. If you get carried away making blocks, even blocks in different color schemes can be combined to make a glorious quilt.

Your Personal Story in a Quilt

Sampler quilts can make wonderful memory quilts, perfect for weddings, anniversaries, and new babies. Fabrics might include remnants from a favorite dress or a familiar apron. Patterns can be chosen to reflect the background and interests of the person who will be using the quilt. I call this kind of quilt a Personal History Sampler.

The vast majority of blocks in *The Block Book* are my own designs, and I made up names that reflect places, hobbies, relations, and other subjects suitable for a Personal History Sampler. You will have fun just looking for blocks that have names meaningful to your loved ones.

Blocks As Folk Art

Blocks can be made into quilts, or they can be the end product. Quilted and bound, or unquilted and framed, blocks are charming home decor for small spaces. A friend has hung a dazzling array of framed blue-and-white blocks to add color above the doors and cupboards in her kitchen.

Block Exchanges: Warm Feelings for "Pin Pals"

Many quilters enjoy exchanging blocks with other quilters. You can make several alike at once for a few friends and get a variety of different blocks in exchange. The blocks from such swaps are often made into sampler quilts that commemorate friendships. These quilts are sure to warm you from head to toe as well as warm your heart.

Blocks Improve Your Skills

If you like planning a quilt and choosing colors and fabrics more than the actual cutting and sewing, you are going to love making and collecting blocks! Furthermore, if you want to gain practice in all areas of quiltmaking, blocks are just the ticket. Making blocks is an excellent way to improve your cutting, sewing, and pressing, to learn new techniques, and to develop your personal style and color use. You don't need to invest much time or material in a block, so if you don't like your results, you can start over. You can learn so much from your mistakes! I have been making quilts for 29 years, and I am still learning. I especially enjoy making blocks to experiment with new fabric styles and colors.

Blocks: Small Squares With Big Potential

Let me digress for a moment. Many quilters have large stashes of fabrics, perhaps too much to ever consider using up in one lifetime. I admit to being one of these fabric collectors. I consider fabric collecting a hobby, as valid as stamp collecting or doll collecting. When I see a fabric I like, I see in it possibilities for quilts. I want to own the fabric to own the possibilities. I understand that I probably won't ever realize all of those possibilities, but they are still there, as are possibilities that I haven't even thought of yet. What a thrill, just knowing that I have all of this wonderful potential in my cupboards!

Recently I have discovered a similar joy in making blocks. A block is potential you can touch. It says, "I could make this quilt," while it gives you the satisfactions of a completed project. What could be better? I can make a block in a half hour or an hour. I can show off to friends the possibilities that I saw, and I still have fabric left for other possibilities!

Give blocks a try. When you view each block as a completed project, it's so easy to feel the thrill of accomplishment.

Please read this before you begin.

For each block there is a photograph, a shaded drawing, a piecing diagram, and a patch list. For every patch, rotary cutting instructions, as well as full-size patterns, are provided at the back of the book. For some blocks, there is also a 9-block drawing to suggest one quilt you might make from the block pattern.

I know that you are eager to start making blocks, so I will keep this brief. There are not very many words in this book. The pictures tell most of the story. Let me explain how to get the most out of the pictures, captions, and charts in this book.

Photographs Excite and Inspire

The color photographs are a great source for color schemes and fabric combinations. Current fabrics were used to make the blocks, but don't feel you must match them exactly. Study the blocks for color ideas. Sometimes, you can use the color scheme from one block with the pattern for another.

Pattern Ratings Help You Choose

Pattern ratings are indicated by stars in front of the block names. You can use the ratings to help you identify the projects that are right for you. I rated patterns from one to three stars, with one star being the easiest. I assigned stars by my gut feeling. Someone else might have different feelings. Don't let a higher rating dissuade you from making any block you desire, even if you are a beginner. After all, it's just one block, you have little to lose, and you may surprise yourself. Most people can tackle anything if their heart is in it. Do be aware of your comfort zone. Some people shy away from lots of pieces or new shapes, which aren't really hard, but they may not be for everyone.

Since there are only three ratings, there is a range of difficulty within each category. I think a cooking analogy might help. Some one-star blocks are like making toast: quick and easy with no experience necessary. Other one-star blocks are like making salad: more ingredients, but they go together quickly. Two star blocks are like meatloaf or a casserole. They take more time, may have more steps, and require following a recipe, but not much can go wrong. Three-star blocks are like apple pie or homemade bread: They take some extra time, but they are worth it. Experience helps, but even a beginner has been known to make a delicate, flaky pie crust or a perfect loaf of bread. You won't find any tricky soufflés or french pastries in this book.

Captions Provide Useful Information

By each block you will find a caption with the pattern rating, name, and the page number for the corresponding diagram or photograph. By the shaded block drawing, you will also find a few words about the origin of the block design and the name of the maker. Finally, there are tips for cutting, piecing, or setting the blocks in a quilt.

Shaded Block Drawings Show Block Details Clearly

These perfectly scaled-down block drawings are suitable for enlarging by photocopy for paper piecing, if desired. However, all blocks can be rotary cut and made in the size listed more easily *without* a foundation. The drawings are shaded to match the block photo wherever possible. Occasionally, I couldn't represent the block's colors perfectly in shades of gray and had to make adjustments. The shading is merely a suggestion. Feel free to change color placement as you see fit.

Diagrams Make the Sewing Easy

By each shaded block drawing is a piecing diagram. A number is assigned to each shape and size of patch. Blocks are exploded to show the first patches joined into subunits and also to show subunits joined to make larger units or rows. Generally, the first patches to be joined are close together, and the later parts are farther and farther apart in the diagram. I recommend cutting precise patches (with a template or with a rotary cutter, whichever you prefer) and sewing as shown. I think you will find my methods accurate, efficient, and appropriate for each block. However, feel free to use any method you desire.

Set-in joints are indicated in the diagrams by a large dot. Don't sew from edge to edge of the patches at these joints. Start sewing at the end of the seamline, ¼" from the raw edge, at the set-in joint. Backtack exactly to the starting point. You will need to remove the work from the sewing machine to push seam allowances aside rather than pivoting at the angle.

Partial seams are indicated by dashed lines in the diagrams. This is an easy alternative to set-ins for some blocks. Stitch halfway down a seam, leaving the dashed end unsewn until later. After adding other units, complete the partial seam.

The Patch List: Your Ingredients

The patch list first gives a number to correspond to the number in the piecing diagram. This is followed by a patch name, such as "S1," which corresponds to the name in the cutting charts and templates in *The Block Book* as well as to the charts in *Judy Martin's Ultimate Rotary Cutting Reference*. This way, you can look up yardage or additional information in that reference, as well.

The patch size comes next. This is the *finished* measurement of the side that is indicated in the rotary cutting figures. Use this finished size to find your patch in the rotary charts and templates, also.

Go to the rotary cutting section starting on page 118 to find the recipe for cutting each shape. If you prefer, go to the template section starting on page 130. Note that cutting charts and templates are in alphabetical order.

Building Blocks for Quilts

Because blocks are the basis for most quilts, I included quilt ideas for many of the blocks. Sketches of a 9-block quilt segment are shown for numerous blocks. Setting suggestions for others are listed in some captions. To make a quilt, you simply make blocks, sew them into rows, and join rows. Sometimes sashes or alternate plain squares are used between blocks. *Judy Martin's Ultimate Rotary Cutting Reference* will help you with yardage figures for your quilt. For an exquisite finishing touch, consider a pieced border. Patterns for 200 borders are presented in *Pieced Borders* by Judy Martin and Marsha McCloskey.

The Grand Blocks on pages 17-25 make wonderful wall quilts or medallion quilt centers. Simply add one or more pieced borders. They also make impressive bed quilts. It takes just a few Grand Blocks set side by side or, perhaps, with sashes. Nine Grand Blocks set 3 x 3 or 16 Grand Blocks set 4 x 4 are usually enough for a queen/king quilt. For a twin, 2 x 3 blocks or 3 x 4 blocks will do. Achieve the exact size desired with the addition of a border.

Important Cutting Information

For details on how to use the cutting charts or templates, go to page 117.

★★★ 32" Dixieland Jazz, p. 17

Original block designed by Judy Martin; made by Diane Tomlinson. A single block makes a stunning medallion center or wall quilt. Find border ideas in *Pieced Borders* by Judy Martin and Marsha McCloskey. If you prefer, set 9 blocks 3 x 3 for a 96" square quilt before borders. Do not fold fabric for D2 or Z7, as no reverses are needed. Note the 8 set-in joints.

Piecing of Star Point

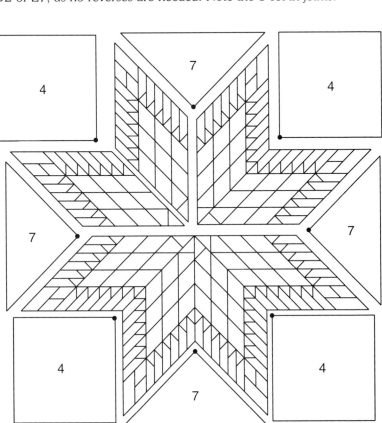

Patch Name	Fin. Size
1. D1	1½"
2. D1	2⅛"
3. D2	1½"
4. S1	9⅜"
5. T1	1½"
6. T1	1+
7. T4	13¼"
8. Z1	1+
9. Z7	2⅛"

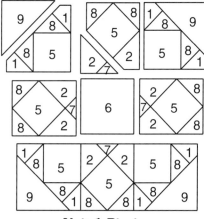

Unit 1 Piecing

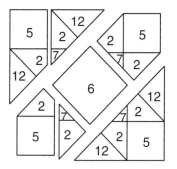

Unit 2 Piecing

★★★ 29" Desert Twilight, p. 17

Original block designed by Judy Martin; made by Chris Hulin. A single block makes a handsome wall quilt, or nine blocks set 3 x 3 make a queen-size quilt. Don't hesitate to make this quilt if you cut and sew precisely. The quilt goes together very simply. However, inaccuracies in cutting and seaming can cause problems when you join units made of small pieces to the large patches. Check your seam gauge for best results.

Patch Name	Fin. Size
1. M9	1¼"
2. M9	1¾"
3. M9	4¼"
4. M9	6"
5. S1	1¾"
6. S1	2½"
7. T1	¾"
8. T1	1¼"
9. T1	2½"
10. T1	4¼"
11. T1	8½"
12. T4	2½"

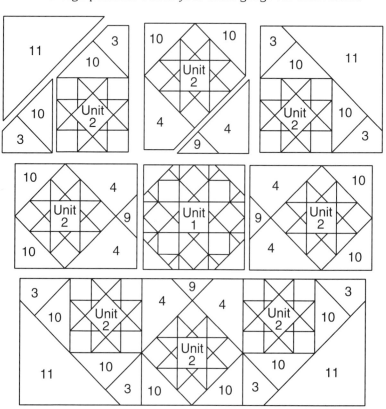

★★ 29" All Star, p. 18

Original block designed and made by Judy Martin. One block makes a wall quilt; nine blocks with sashing make a queen- or king-size quilt. Note that all Z9 patches are reversed. Cut them as shown for Z9 on page 128, but with the fabric face down. Do not fold fabric for Z9r or Z7 patches.

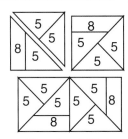

Pinwheel Unit

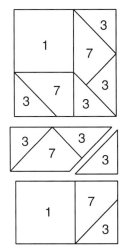

Half Star Unit

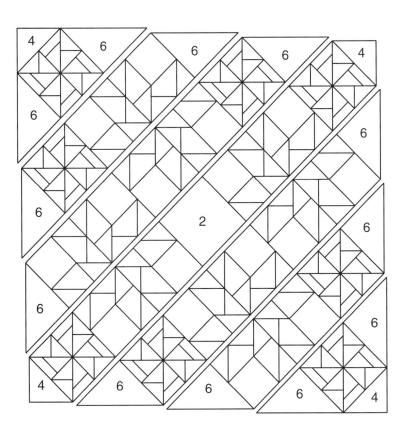

Patch Name	Fin. Size
1. S1	3"
2. S1	5⅛"
3. T1	2⅛"
4. T1	3⅝"
5. T4	2½+
6. T4	7¼"
7. Z7	3"
8. Z9r	2½+

★★★ 24¾" Flying Swallows Variation, p. 18

The block center is a traditional Flying Swallows. Judy Martin added the wreath of partial stars to make a new block variation. The block was made by Jane Bazyn. Make a one-block wall quilt or make a queen-sized quilt from 9 blocks set 3 x 3 with a wide border. This block is made from simple shapes. However, there are many set-in patches, making this a challenging, but beautiful, project.

Patch Name	Fin. Size
1. D1	2⅛"
2. S2	4¼"
3. T1	7¼"
4. T4	3"
5. T4	7¼"

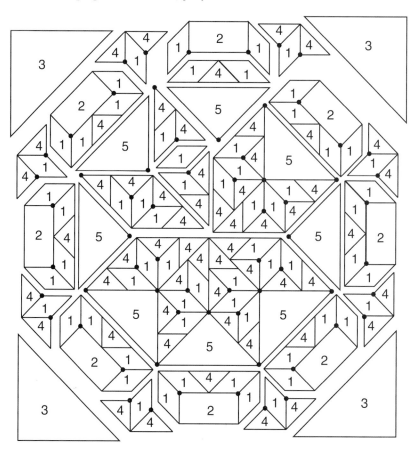

★★ 24" Dovetails, p. 19

Original block designed by Judy Martin; made by Jean Nolte. Traditional Rising Stars and Evening Stars are combined in an exciting new arrangement in this new block. One block makes an attractive wall hanging. Twelve blocks make a twin quilt and sixteen blocks make a queen/king quilt. In the bigger quilts you can turn blocks for Log Cabin-like set variations. See nine Dovetails blocks set side by side on page 14.

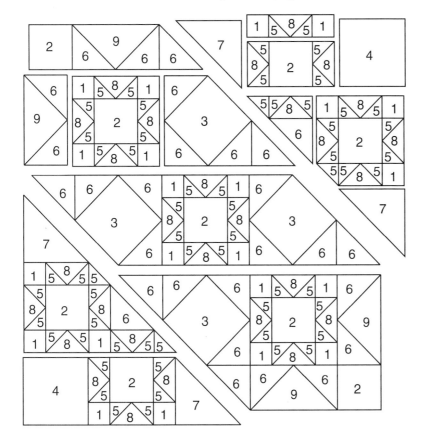

Patch Name	Fin. Size
1. S1	1½"
2. S1	3"
3. S1	4¼"
4. S1	4½"
5. T1	1½"
6. T1	3"
7. T1	4½"
8. T4	3"
9. T4	6"

**Dovetails
Quilt Section,
p. 13**

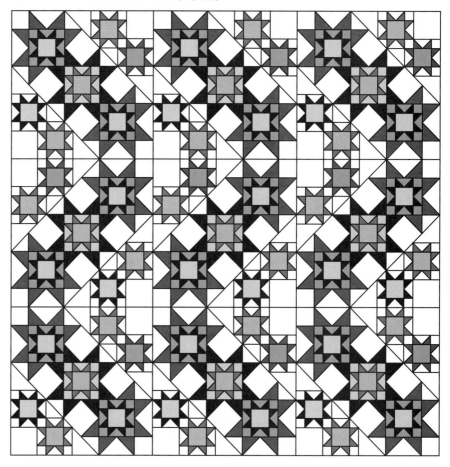

**Starry, Starry Night
Quilt Section,
p. 15**

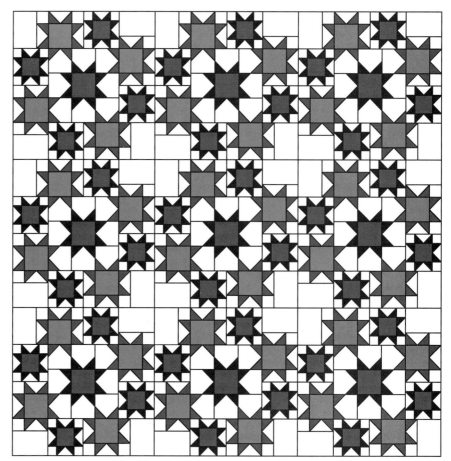

★ **24" Starry, Starry Night, p. 19**

Original block designed and made by Judy Martin. Simple shapes combine to make familiar Evening Stars in two sizes. The unique arrangement adds a circular movement to the design. Make a small wall quilt from a single block framed with a Sawtooth triangle border. Set side by side, 12 blocks set 3 x 4 make a twin quilt and 16 blocks set 4 x 4 make a king-size quilt. See the 3 x 3 quilt segment on page 14.

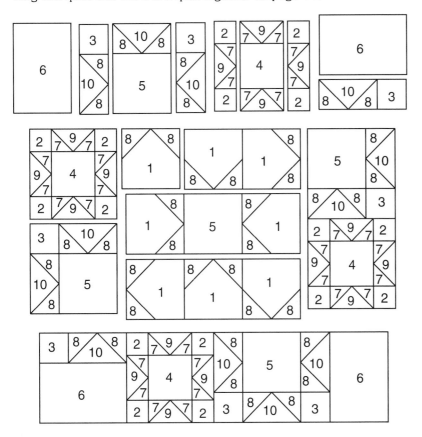

Patch Name	Fin. Size
1. P9	4"
2. S1	1½"
3. S1	2"
4. S1	3"
5. S1	4"
6. S13	6"
7. T1	1½"
8. T1	2"
9. T4	3"
10. T4	4"

★★ 24" Barbershop Quartet, p. 20

Original block designed and made by Judy Martin. This block was inspired by the traditional Rising Star pattern, with a star within a star. Here, the Rising Star becomes the center of a bigger star yet. The small center star repeats in the block corners. Nine blocks set 3 x 3 with sashes make a queen-size quilt. A border of small stars would be attractive.

Patch Name	Fin. Size
1. S1	1½"
2. S1	3"
3. T1	1½"
4. T1	3"
5. T1	6"
6. T4	3"
7. T4	6"
8. T4	12"

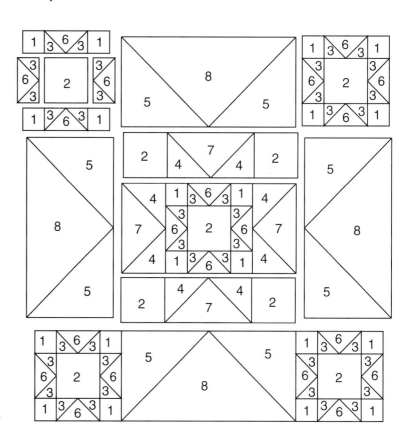

★★★ 32"
Dixieland Jazz
p. 9

★★★ 29"
Desert Twilight
p. 10

★★ 29"
All Star
p. 11

★★★ 24¾"
Flying Swallows
Variation
p. 12

★★ 24"
Dovetails
p. 13

★ 24"
Starry, Starry Night
p. 15

★★ 24"
Barbershop Quartet
p. 16

★★ 24"
Kentucky Star
p. 49

★ 24"
Five-Star Block
p. 50

★ 24"
Firelight Nights
p. 52

★ 24"
Star-Spangled Quilt
p. 53

★★★ 21¼"
New England Beauty
p. 55

★★★ 20½"
Chicago Blues
p. 56

★★★ 20½"
Fountain of Youth
p. 57

★★★ 20½"
Rio Grande
p. 58

★★ 20½"
Snow Crystals
Variation
p. 59

★ 18"
Home Fires Burning
p. 60

★★★ 17½"
Shipshewana Star
p. 61

★ 12" Judy's Star, p. 62

★ 12" Martha Washington's Star, p. 62

★ 12" Rising Star, p. 62

★ 12" Rising Star, p. 63

★★ 12" The Bard of Avon, p. 63

★★ 12" Shelburne Star, p. 63

★★ 12" Some Enchanted Evening, p. 64

★ 12" The City of New Orleans, p. 64

★ 12" Island Music, p. 64

★★ 12" Blackford's Beauty, p. 65

★★ 12" Autumn Splendor, p. 65

★★ 12" Bear Hugs, p. 65

★★ 12" Promises to Keep, p. 66

★★ 12" Empire State, p. 66

★★ 12" Baby Blue, p. 66

★★ 12" Happy-Go-Lucky, p. 67

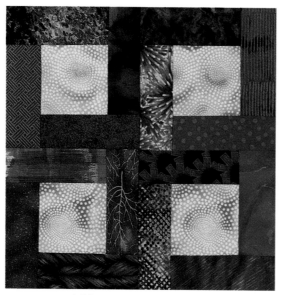

★ 12" Bright Hopes, p. 67

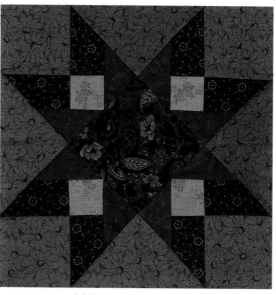

★ 12" June Bride, p. 67

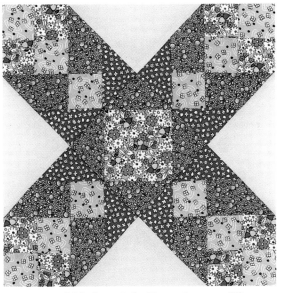

★★ 12" Auntie's Favorite, p. 68

★ 12" Needles & Pins, p. 68

★ 12" The Romantic Age, p. 68

★★★ 12" Green Mountain Star, p. 69

★ 12" Village Green, p. 69

★★ 12" Fall Classic, p. 69

★ 12" Brotherly Love, p. 70

★ 12" Navajo, p. 70

★★ 12" Ocean Waves, p. 70

★★ 12" The Rambler, p. 71

★ 12" Virginia Backroads, p. 71

★★ 12" Born Under a Wandering Star, p. 72

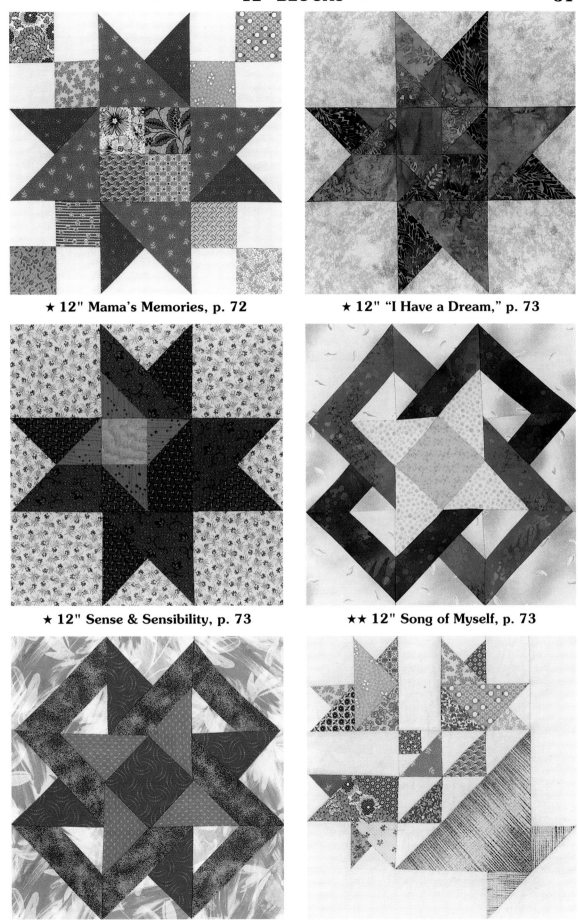

★ 12" Mama's Memories, p. 72

★ 12" "I Have a Dream," p. 73

★ 12" Sense & Sensibility, p. 73

★★ 12" Song of Myself, p. 73

★★ 12" Land of the Midnight Sun, p. 74

★★ 12" Carolina Basket, p. 74

★★ 12" Robbing Peter to Pay Paul, p. 74

★★ 12" Cyberstar, p. 75

★★ 12" Ragtime, p. 75

★★ 12" Prairie Star Basket, p. 75

★ 12" Costa del Sol, p. 76

★★ 12" Football Star, p. 76

★★ 12" Country Boy, p. 77

★★ 12" Covered Bridge, p. 77

★★ 12" Cross Roads to Texas, p. 77

★ 12" Sailing by the Stars, p. 78

★ 12" Diamond Head, p. 78

★★★ 12" Victoria Station, p. 79

★★ 12" The River Jordan, p. 79

★ 12" Twisting Star, p. 80

★ 12" Tropical Breeze, p. 80

★★ 12" Concord Hymn, p. 80

★★ 12" Road to Fortune, p. 81

★★ 12" The Silk Road, p. 81

★ 12" Night & Day Variation, p. 82

★ 12" Arabian Nights, p. 82

★ 12" Olympic Mountain Star, p. 82

★★ 12" Bridge of Sighs, p. 83

★★ 12" Vintage Star, p. 83

★★ 12" Aztec Star, p. 84

★★ 12" Palm Sunday, p. 84

★★ 12" Macintosh Block, p. 85

★★ 12" Oliver Twist, p. 85

★★ 12" A Red, Red Rose, p. 86

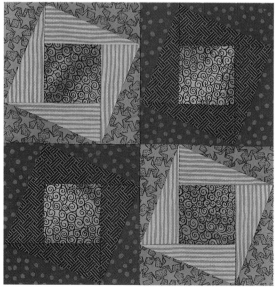

★★ 12" Whodunit, p. 86

★★ 12" Strikes & Spares, p. 86

★★ 10¼" LeMoyne Star, p. 87

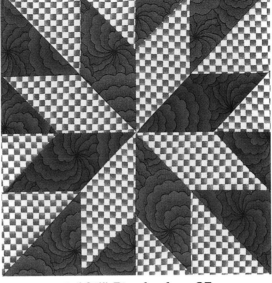

★ 10¼" Pinwheel, p. 87

★★★ 10¼" Angels on High, p. 87

★★★ 10¼" Diamonds Are Forever, p. 88

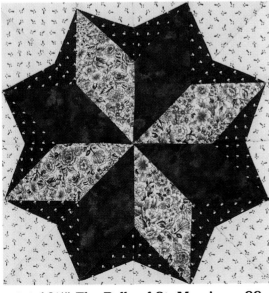

★★ 10¼" The Bells of St. Mary's, p. 88

★★ 10¼" Liberty Bell, p. 89

★★ 10¼" North Country Fair, p. 89

★★★ 10¼" Niagara Star, p. 89

★★★ 10¼" Arts & Crafts, p. 90

★★★ 10¼" Des Moines Star, p. 90

★★ 10¼" Salsa, p. 90

★★ 10¼" Writer's Block, p. 91

★★ 10¼" Irish Eyes, p. 91

★ 10¼" Coventry Carol, p. 91

★★ 10¼" Song of Solomon, p. 92

★★ 10¼" Constitution Block, p. 92

★★ 10¼" St. Joan's Star, p. 92

★★ 10¼" Delft Star, p. 93

★ 10¼" Millennium, p. 93

★★ 10¼" Band of Gold, p. 93

★ 10¼" Kansas City, p. 94

★★ 10¼" Chantilly Lace, p. 94

★★ 10¼" The Holy Land, p. 94

★★ 10¼" Victory Garden, p. 95

★★ 10¼" **Silver Threads & Golden Needles, p. 95**

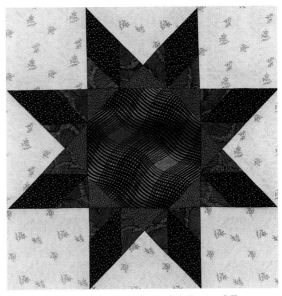

★★ 10¼" **August Block, p. 95**

★ 10¼" **Amber Waves, p. 96**

★★ 10¼" **Home Improvement, p. 96**

★ 10¼" **The Night Watch, p. 96**

★★ 10¼" **Graceland, p. 97**

★★ 10¼" Chincoteague Mist, p. 97

★★ 10¼" A Midsummer Night's Dream, p. 97

★★ 10¼" Tivoli Gardens, p. 98

★ 10¼" Jabberwocky, p. 98

★★ 10¼" Sun & Sea, p. 98

★★ 10¼" Midnight Ride, p. 99

★★10¼" Penny Lane, p. 99

★★ 10¼" Oregon Coast, p. 99

★★ 10¼" National Champion, p. 100

★★ 10¼" Paper of Pins, p. 100

★ 10¼" Bluegrass Block, p. 100

★★ 10¼" Texas Twister, p. 101

★★★ 10¼" The Rain in Spain, p. 101

★★★ 10¼" Twist & Shout, p. 101

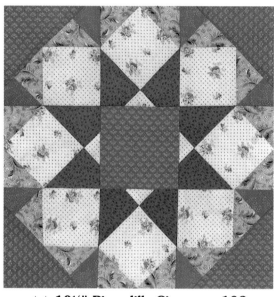

★★ 10¼" Piccadilly Circus, p. 102

★ 10¼" Diamond Jubilee, p. 102

★ 10¼" Pinwheel, p. 103

★ 10" Evening Star, p. 103

★ 10" Burnham Square Variation, p. 103

★ 10" Sister's Choice, p. 104

★ 10" Father's Day, p. 104

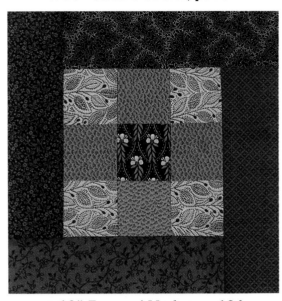

★ 10" Farmers' Market, p. 104

★ 10" Kutztown Puzzle, p. 105

★ 10" Cross & Crown, p. 105

★★ 10" Independence Day, p. 106

★★ 10" Grandma's Scrapbook, p. 106

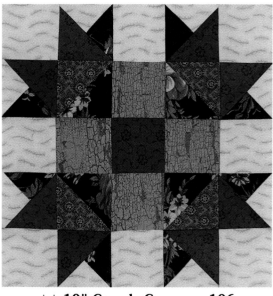

★★ 10" Canada Goose, p. 106

★ 10" Grape Basket, p. 107

★ 10" Appalachian Basket, p. 107

★ 10" Stitcher's Square, p. 107

★ 10" Elementary Block, p. 108

★★ 10" Domino & Squares, p. 108

★ 10" Streets of Laredo, p. 109

★ 10" Log Cabin, p. 109

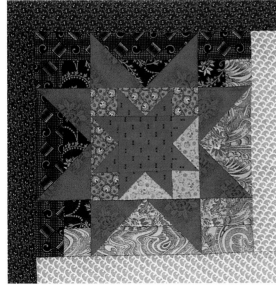

★★ 10" Great Lakes Log Cabin, p. 110

★★ 15" Across the Wide Missouri, p. 110

★★★ 14" Goose Tracks, p. 111

★★ 14" Bluebells, p. 111

★★ 13¼" Prairie Patchwork, p. 111

★ 9" Measure for Measure, p. 112

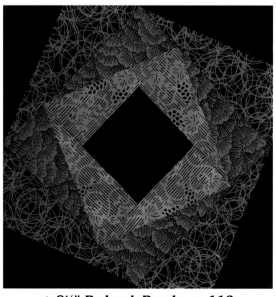

★ 8½" Paducah Puzzle, p. 112

★ 8½" Sydney Star, p. 112

★★ **24" Kentucky Star, p. 20**

This original block, designed by Judy Martin, includes a traditional Kentucky Crossroads block (also known as Cross Roads to Texas) in the center of the star. It was made by Margy Sieck. It is suitable for a one-block wall quilt, a nine-block quilt set with sashes, or a twelve- or sixteen-block twin- or king-size quilt of blocks set side by side.

Patch Name	Fin. Size
1. S1	1⅜+
2. S1	4½"
3. S3	4¼"
4. T1	1⅜+
5. T1	1½"
6. T1	3"
7. T1	6"
8. T4	6"
9. T4	8"

Note: For perfect results, when you rotary cut patches #1 and #4, cut them a thread's width smaller than the listed size, which was rounded up very slightly. Compare your patches to the full-size templates on pages 133 and 138, which are perfect.

★ 24" Five-Star Block, p. 21

Original block designed by Judy Martin; made by Margy Sieck. This block is similar to the next two blocks. Look at those, as well, for color ideas. This block is made from a center square unit and four rectangular units. Note that the first rectangular unit is attached to the center unit with a partial seam. Subsequent rectangular units are added before the partial seam is completed. See the quilt segment on page 51.

Patch Name	Fin. Size
1. P9	4"
2. S1	2"
3. S1	4"
4. S3	6"
5. S3	12"
6. T1	2"
7. T4	4"

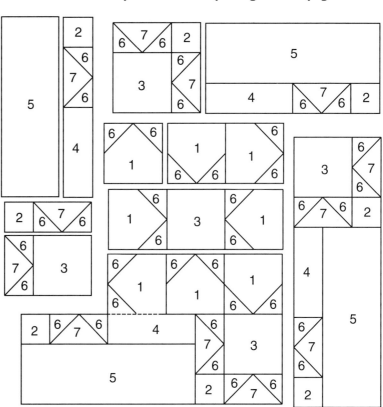

**Five-Star Block
Quilt Section,
p. 50**

**Firelight Nights
Quilt Section,
p. 52**

★ 24" Firelight Nights, p. 21

Original block designed by Judy Martin; made by Chris Hulin. Join patches as shown in the diagram to make a center square and four rectangular units. Sew the first unit to the center square with a partial seam, stitching only halfway down the seamline. Attach the remaining units before completing the partial seam. Arrange blocks as shown on page 51.

Patch Name	Fin. Size
1. P9	4"
2. S1	2"
3. S1	4"
4. T1	2"
5. T4	4"

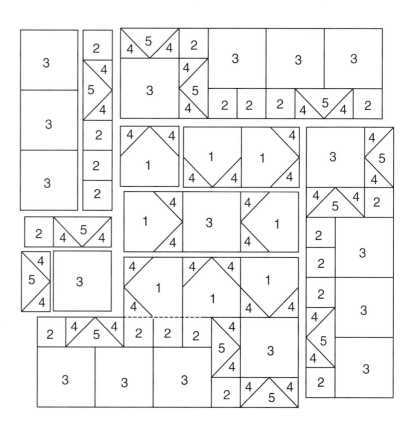

★ 24" Star-Spangled Quilt, p. 22

Original block designed by Judy Martin; made by Jean Nolte. Join patches as shown in the diagram to make a center square and four rectangular units. Sew the first unit to the center square with a partial seam, stitching only halfway down the seamline. Attach the remaining units before completing the partial seam. Arrange blocks as shown on page 54.

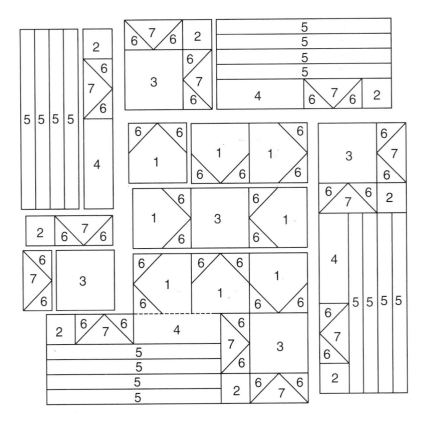

Patch Name	Fin. Size
1. P9	4"
2. S1	2"
3. S1	4"
4. S3	6"
5. S12	12"
6. T1	2"
7. T4	4"

Star-Spangled Quilt
Quilt Section,
p. 53

New England Beauty
Quilt Section,
p. 55

★★★ 21¼" New England Beauty, p. 22

Original block designed and made by Judy Martin. Cut D1/D1r and T8/T8r from folded fabric. D1 and T8 shapes are actually symmetrical, but cutting mirror images will enable you to place straight grain all around the block's edges. Stack unfolded medium and dark fabrics face to face with dark face down to cut T9/T9r. Set blocks side by side as shown on page 54. Just 16 blocks set 4 x 4 make a queen-sized quilt.

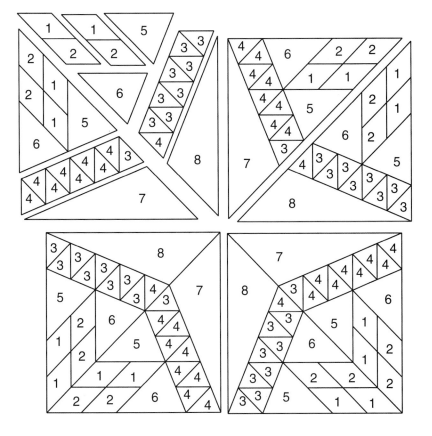

Patch Name	Fin. Size
1. D1	2⅛"
2. D1r	2⅛"
3. T8	2⅛"
4. T8r	2⅛"
5. T8	4¼"
6. T8r	4¼"
7. T9	10⅝"
8. T9r	10⅝"

Note: In order to keep straight grain around the edges of the units, D1 and D1r are separate entries. They differ only in grain. The same is true of T8 and T8r. If you wish to ignore the grain, you may cut D1 for both D1 and D1r and cut T8 for both T8 and T8r.

★★★ 20½" Chicago Blues, p. 23

Original block designed and made by Judy Martin. Frame a single block with pieced borders for a wall quilt that will show off your best quilting. Twelve or sixteen blocks set with sashing make a bed quilt. Fold fabric to cut D1 and D1r at the same time and also to cut 1½" T8 and T8r patches. Cut the 6" T8r's from face-down fabric. Note the 8 set-in joints.

Patch Name	Fin. Size
1. D1	1½"
2. D1r	1½"
3. S1	6"
4. T4	8½"
5. T8	1½"
6. T8r	1½"
7. T8r	6"

Note: In order to keep straight grain around the edges of the units, D1 and D1r are separate entries. They differ only in grain. The same is true of T8 and T8r. If you wish to ignore the grain, you may cut D1 for both D1 and D1r and cut T8 for both T8 and T8r.

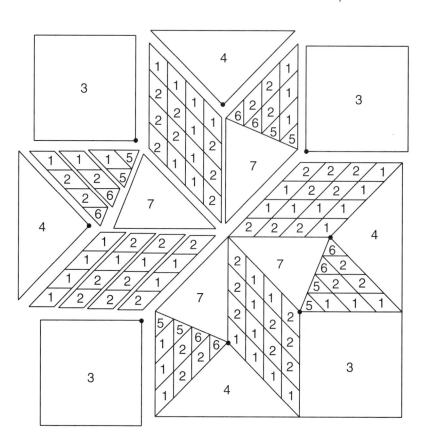

★★★ 20½" Fountain of Youth, p. 23

Original block designed by Judy Martin; made by Chris Hulin. Fountain of Youth combines Lone Star and Feathered Star components in an impressive, new star. Four by four blocks set with sashing make a king-sized quilt. One block makes a memorable wallhanging. Note the 8 set-in joints.

Patch Name	Fin. Size
1. D1	3"
2. S1	1½"
3. S1	3"
4. T1	1½"
5. T4	4¼"

★★★ 20½" Rio Grande, p. 24

Original block designed by Judy Martin; made by Jane Bazyn. Sixteen blocks set side by side in four rows of four make a terrific queen/king quilt. Small stars form where blocks touch, and the half stars ring the bigger star, adding a circular movement. This block has 32 set-in joints, so it is not for the faint of heart. But as you can see, it is well worth the effort.

Patch Name	Fin. Size
1. D1	1½"
2. D1	1¾"
3. D1	3"
4. D2	1½"
5. S1	1¾"
6. T1	6"
7. T4	2½"

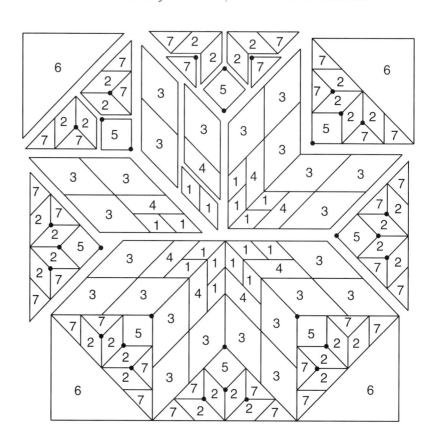

★★ **20½" Snow Crystals Variation, p. 24**

This is a traditional block with seams added to eliminate set-ins and add background texture. It was made by Margy Sieck. It makes a handsome medallion quilt center. Like any of the 20½" blocks, it can be substituted for four 10¼" blocks in a sampler quilt of blocks set side by side.

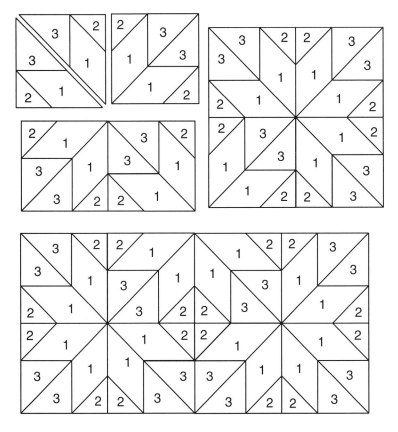

Patch Name	Fin. Size
1. D1	3"
2. T1	2⅛"
3. T1	3"

★ **18" Home Fires Burning, p. 25**

Original block designed and made by Judy Martin. Familiar squares and triangles combine here for a new pattern. Sixteen blocks set with sashing make a queen-size quilt. Just twelve blocks make a quilt for a twin bed. Large patches make quick work of this block and provide a good place to embellish with quilting.

Patch Name	Fin. Size
1. S1	1½"
2. S1	2⅛"
3. S1	3"
4. S1	4½"
5. T1	1½"
6. T1	4½"
7. T4	3"
8. T4	9"

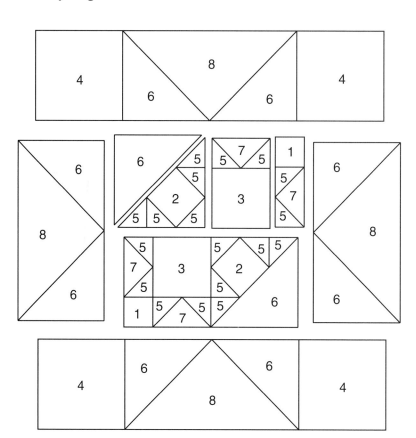

★★★ 17½" Shipshewana Star, p. 25

Original block designed and made by Judy Martin. Diamonds both bold and subtle make the small stars dance and sparkle over the surface of the larger star. This block was inspired by the traditional Flying Swallows block, and it is equally challenging to make with its many set-in joints. If you love the look, why not take this opportunity to master set-ins? You will be glad you did!

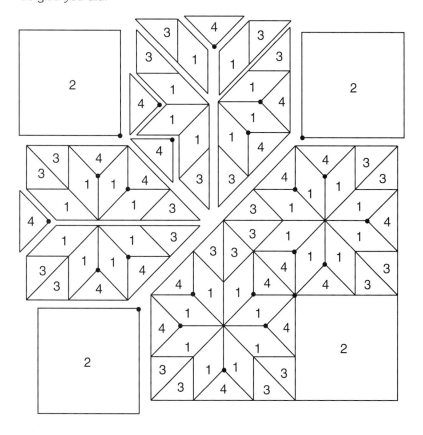

Patch Name	Fin. Size
1. D1	2⅛"
2. S1	5⅛"
3. T1	2⅛"
4. T4	3"

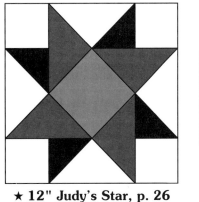

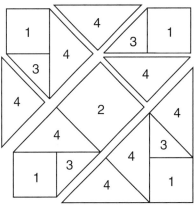

★ **12" Judy's Star, p. 26**

Patch Name	Fin. Size
1. S1	3"
2. S1	4¼"
3. T1	3"
4. T4	6"

Or (6" block):

1. S1	1½"
2. S1	2⅛"
3. T1	1½"
4. T4	3"

Original block designed by Judy Martin; reprinted from *Judy Martin's Ultimate Book of Quilt Block Patterns*; made by Patsy Carr. This one is little different from the usual star and just as easy! Make a twin-sized quilt from 30 blocks set 5 x 6 with 2" or 3" sashes.

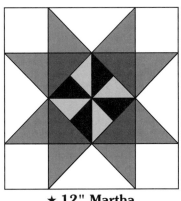

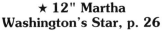

★ **12" Martha Washington's Star, p. 26**

Patch Name	Fin. Size
1. S1	3"
2. T1	2⅛"
3. T1	3"
4. T4	6"

Traditional block made by Diane Tomlinson. Make a queen-sized quilt from 36 blocks set 6 x 6 with 3" sashes. For a twin-sized quilt, you will need just 30 blocks set 5 x 6 with 2-3" sashes.

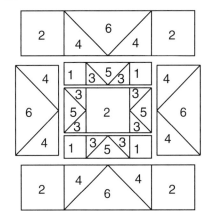

★ **12" Rising Star, p. 26**

Patch Name	Fin. Size
1. S1	1½"
2. S1	3"
3. T1	1½"
4. T1	3"
5. T4	3"
6. T4	6"

Traditional block made by Judy Martin. For a queen-sized quilt, you will need 25 blocks and 24 alternate plain squares. Alternate them in a set of 7 x 7 blocks or squares. Add a pieced or quilted border. Quilt a pretty motif in the alternate plain squares.

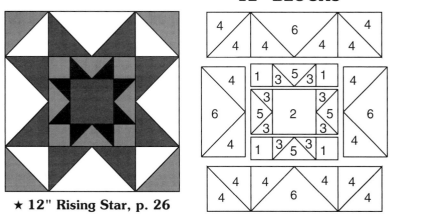

★ **12" Rising Star, p. 26**

Patch Name	Fin. Size
1. S1	1½"
2. S1	3"
3. T1	1½"
4. T1	3"
5. T4	3"
6. T4	6"

Traditional block made by Rebecca Loew. This differs from the other Rising Star in having corner triangles instead of squares. Arrange 30 blocks 5 x 6 with 3" sashes for a twin-sized quilt. For a queen-sized quilt, you will need 36 blocks set 6 x 6 with 3" sashes.

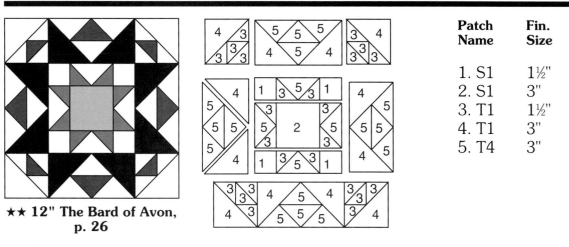

★★ **12" The Bard of Avon, p. 26**

Patch Name	Fin. Size
1. S1	1½"
2. S1	3"
3. T1	1½"
4. T1	3"
5. T4	3"

Original block designed and made by Judy Martin. This was inspired by a traditional Rising Star combined with an adaptation of the ring of triangles from Marsha McCloskey's Italian Tile block. 36 blocks set six by six with 3" sashes make a lovely queen-sized quilt.

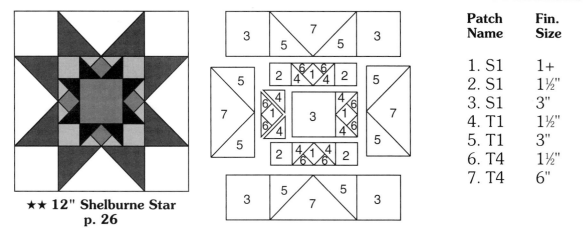

★★ **12" Shelburne Star p. 26**

Patch Name	Fin. Size
1. S1	1+
2. S1	1½"
3. S1	3"
4. T1	1½"
5. T1	3"
6. T4	1½"
7. T4	6"

Original block designed and made by Judy Martin. Alternate 25 Shelburne Star blocks with 24 plain squares in a 7 x 7 set. Add borders for a handsome queen-sized quilt. For a twin-sized quilt, you will need 18 blocks and 17 plain squares alternating in a 5 x 7 set.

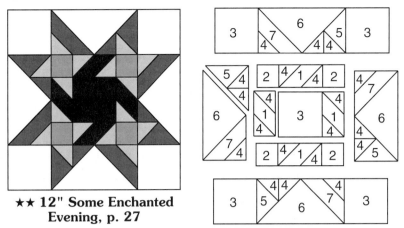

★★ 12" Some Enchanted Evening, p. 27

Patch Name	Fin. Size
1. D3r	1½"
2. S1	1½"
3. S1	3"
4. T1	1½"
5. T4	3"
6. T4	6"
7. Z1	1½"

Original block designed and made by Judy Martin. This is one of several new blocks in *The Block Book* having stars superimposed on stars. Set 6 x 6 with 1½" sashes, and a wide border, 36 blocks make a queen-sized quilt. Cut D3r from face-down fabric.

★ 12" The City of New Orleans, p. 27

Patch Name	Fin. Size
1. S1	1½"
2. S1	3"
3. S2	3"
4. T1	1½"
5. T4	6"
6. Z1	1½"

Original block designed and made by Judy Martin. A good contrast between medium and dark and medium and light helps here. Here is another superimposed effect. Arrange 36 blocks in 6 rows of 6 with 3" sashes for a queen- or king-sized quilt.

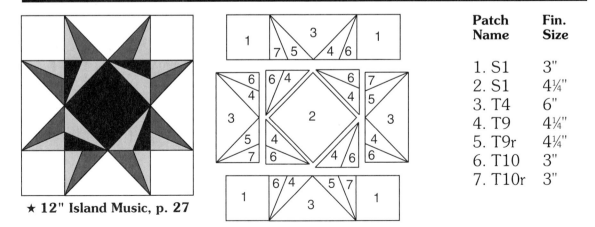

★ 12" Island Music, p. 27

Patch Name	Fin. Size
1. S1	3"
2. S1	4¼"
3. T4	6"
4. T9	4¼"
5. T9r	4¼"
6. T10	3"
7. T10r	3"

Original block designed by Judy Martin; made by Chris Hulin. This is a good block for using shaded effects or bright accents. Cut light T10/T10r as well as medium T9/T9r from folded fabric. Cut remaining patches from unfolded fabric. Arrange blocks alternately with plain squares in 7 rows of 7 for a queen-sized quilt.

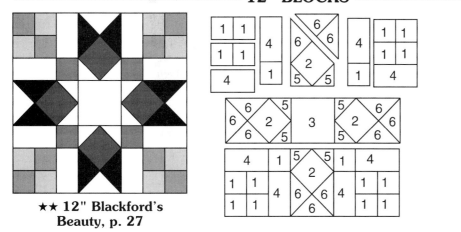

Patch Name	Fin. Size
1. S1	1½"
2. S1	2⅛"
3. S1	3"
4. S2	3"
5. T1	1½"
6. T4	3"

★★ 12" Blackford's Beauty, p. 27

Traditional block made by Diane Tomlinson. For a king-sized quilt set with 1½" sashes, you will need 49 blocks in 7 rows of 7. For a twin quilt, you will need 30 blocks set 5 x 6 with 1½" sashes.

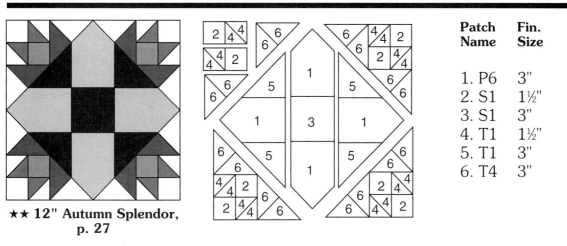

Patch Name	Fin. Size
1. P6	3"
2. S1	1½"
3. S1	3"
4. T1	1½"
5. T1	3"
6. T4	3"

★★ 12" Autumn Splendor, p. 27

Original block designed by Judy Martin; made by Dorothy Palmer. Arrange 36 blocks in 6 rows of 6 with 3" sashes between blocks. This makes an elegant queen-sized quilt. Just 20 blocks set 4 x 5 with 3" sashes and a wide border make a twin-sized quilt.

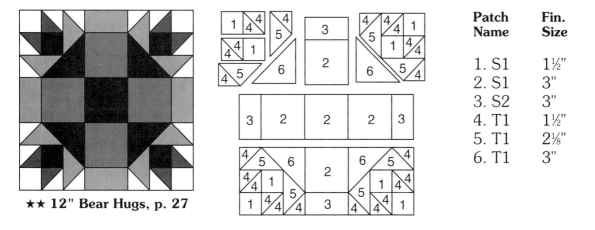

Patch Name	Fin. Size
1. S1	1½"
2. S1	3"
3. S2	3"
4. T1	1½"
5. T1	2⅛"
6. T1	3"

★★ 12" Bear Hugs, p. 27

Original block designed and made by Judy Martin. The coloring from the Autumn Splendor block, above, is also good here. A king-sized quilt can be made from 49 blocks set 7 x 7 with 1½" sashes.

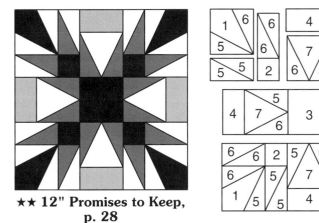

★★ **12" Promises to Keep,**
p. 28

Patch Name	Fin. Size
1. M8	1½"
2. S1	1½"
3. S1	3"
4. S2	3"
5. T13	3"
6. T13r	3"
7. T14	3"

Original block designed by Judy Martin; made by Chris Hulin. Set blocks side by side to create a secondary pattern of four-pointed stars at the block junctures. Cut T13r as you cut T13 from folded fabric. For a queen-sized quilt, arrange 49 blocks in 7 rows of 7.

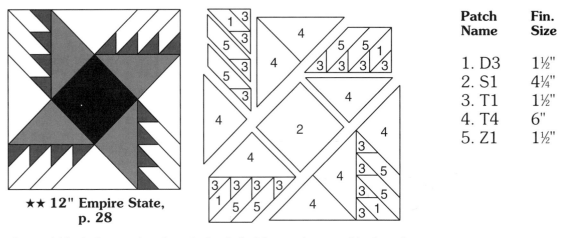

★★ **12" Empire State,**
p. 28

Patch Name	Fin. Size
1. D3	1½"
2. S1	4¼"
3. T1	1½"
4. T4	6"
5. Z1	1½"

Original block designed and made by Judy Martin. Arrange blocks side by side in 8 rows of 8 for a king-sized quilt. For a twin quilt, 24 blocks set 4 x 6 with 1½" sashes and a border would be attractive.

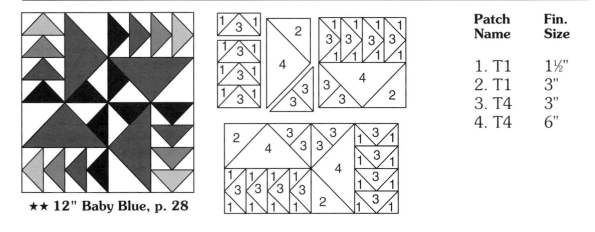

★★ **12" Baby Blue, p. 28**

Patch Name	Fin. Size
1. T1	1½"
2. T1	3"
3. T4	3"
4. T4	6"

Original block designed and made by Judy Martin. This block is delightful set side by side, although the points around the edges are easier to handle when 1½" sashes are used. Either way, 49 blocks set 7 x 7 with a border make a queen- or king-sized quilt.

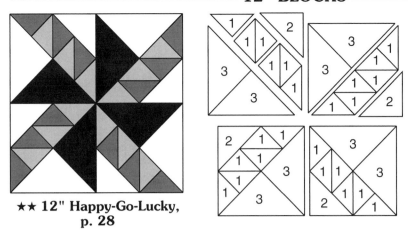

★★ 12" Happy-Go-Lucky, p. 28

Patch Name	Fin. Size
1. T1	2⅛"
2. T1	3"
3. T4	6"

Original block designed by Judy Martin; reprinted from *Judy Martin's Ultimate Book of Quilt Block Patterns*; made by Jane Bazyn. You will need 36 blocks set 6 x 6 with 3" sashes for a queen-sized quilt.

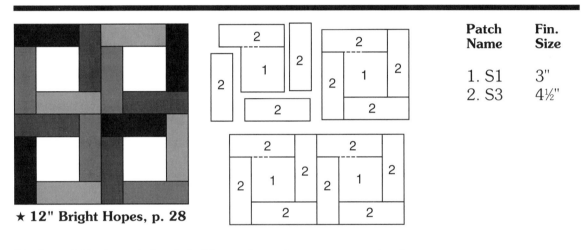

★ 12" Bright Hopes, p. 28

Patch Name	Fin. Size
1. S1	3"
2. S3	4½"

Traditional block made by Judy Martin. In each quarter, sew the first rectangle to the square with a partial seam, stitching only halfway down the seamline. Add the remaining three rectangles before completing the partial seam. Use scraps and set blocks side by side for a great quilt.

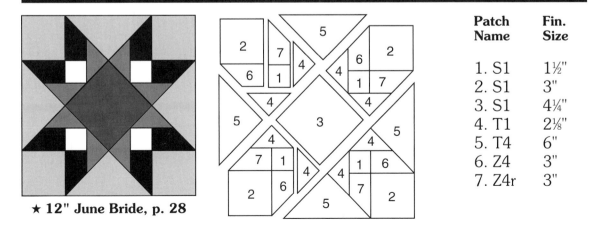

★ 12" June Bride, p. 28

Patch Name	Fin. Size
1. S1	1½"
2. S1	3"
3. S1	4¼"
4. T1	2⅛"
5. T4	6"
6. Z4	3"
7. Z4r	3"

Original block designed by Judy Martin; reprinted from *Judy Martin's Ultimate Book of Quilt Block Patterns*; made by Diane Tomlinson. Cut Z4r as you cut Z4 from folded fabric. Make a full-sized quilt from 42 blocks set 6 x 7 with 1½" sashes.

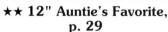
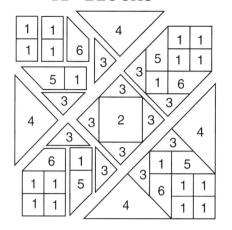

★★ **12" Auntie's Favorite,**
p. 29

Patch Name	Fin. Size
1. S1	1½"
2. S1	3"
3. T1	2⅛"
4. T4	6"
5. Z4	3"
6. Z4r	3"

Original block designed by Judy Martin; reprinted from *Judy Martin's Ultimate Book of Quilt Block Patterns;* made by Margy Sieck. Cut Z4r as you cut Z4 from folded fabric. Set blocks in 6 rows of 6 with 1½"-wide sashes. 36 blocks make a queen quilt.

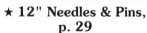
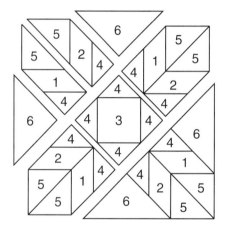

★ **12" Needles & Pins,**
p. 29

Patch Name	Fin. Size
1. D4	3"
2. D4r	3"
3. S1	3"
4. T1	2⅛"
5. T1	3"
6. T4	6"

Original block designed by Judy Martin; reprinted from her *Patchworkbook;* made by Jean Nolte. Cut D4 and D4r from face-to-face dark and medium fabrics with the medium fabric face down. Set 30 blocks 5 x 6 with 3" sashes for a twin quilt.

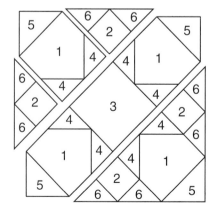

★ **12" The Romantic Age,**
p. 29

Patch Name	Fin. Size
1. P9	4¼"
2. S1	2⅛"
3. S1	4¼"
4. T1	2⅛"
5. T1	3"
6. T4	3"

Original block designed and made by Judy Martin. Set blocks with 2" sashes between them. You will need 36 blocks arranged in 6 rows of 6 for a queen-sized quilt.

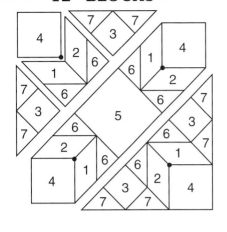

Patch Name	Fin. Size
1. D4	3"
2. D4r	3"
3. S1	2⅛"
4. S1	3"
5. S1	4¼"
6. T1	2⅛"
7. T4	3"

★★★ **12" Green Mountain Star, p. 29**

Original block designed by Judy Martin; reprinted from her *Patchworkbook*; made by Diane Tomlinson. Note the set-in joints. Cut D4/D4r from folded fabric. Frame blocks with 1"-wide strips and set with 2" sashes between blocks. 25 blocks set 5 x 5 make a queen quilt.

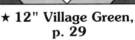

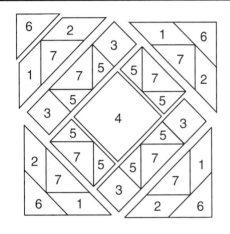

Patch Name	Fin. Size
1. D4	3"
2. D4r	3"
3. S1	2⅛"
4. S1	4¼"
5. T1	2⅛"
6. T1	3"
7. T4	4¼"

★ **12" Village Green, p. 29**

Original block designed by Judy Martin; reprinted from Judy's book, *Scraps, Blocks & Quilts;* made by Diane Tomlinson. Cut D4r as you cut D4 from folded fabric. Set with 3" sashes and setting squares to match the corner triangles. 36 blocks set 6 x 6 make a queen quilt.

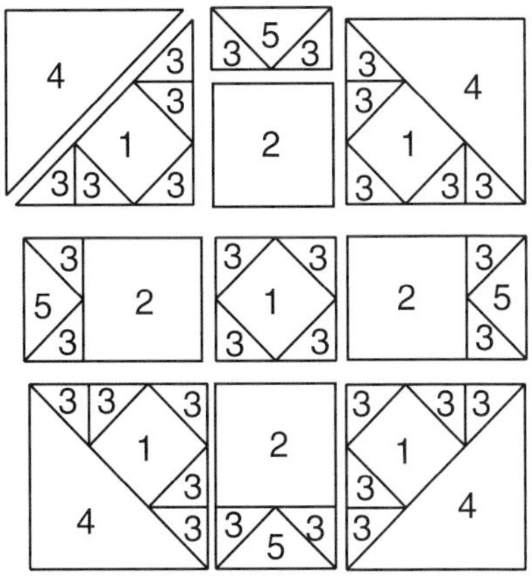

Patch Name	Fin. Size
1. S1	2⅛"
2. S1	3"
3. T1	1½"
4. T1	4½"
5. T4	3"

★★ **12" Fall Classic, p. 29**

Original block designed and made by Judy Martin. Set blocks side by side or with 1½" sashes between them. Either way, 49 blocks set 7 x 7 make a queen-sized quilt. Add a pieced border, if desired. Many appropriate border patterns are in Martin and McCloskey's *Pieced Borders.*

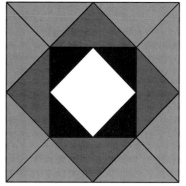
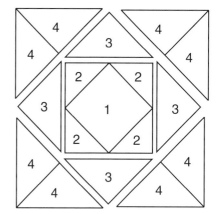

★ **12" Brotherly Love,**
p. 30

Patch Name	Fin. Size
1. S1	4¼"
2. T1	3"
3. T1	4¼"
4. T4	6"

Or (6" block):

1. S1	2⅛"
2. T1	1½"
3. T1	2⅛"
4. T4	3"

Original block designed by Judy Martin; reprinted from *Judy Martin's Ultimate Book of Quilt Block Patterns;* made by Janet Westberg. Careful cutting makes mitered stripes easy here. Set 25 blocks alternately with 24 plain squares in 7 rows of 7 for a queen-sized quilt.

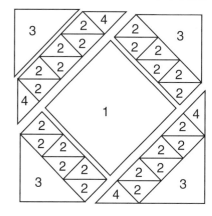

★ **12" Navajo, p. 30**

Patch Name	Fin. Size
1. S1	6⅜"
2. T1	2⅛"
3. T1	4½"
4. T4	3"

Traditional block made by Sharon Jolly. For an easy twin-sized quilt, alternate 18 blocks with 17 plain squares in 7 rows of 5. For a finishing touch, add a dogtooth border of triangles to match those in the block. Find this border pattern in *Pieced Borders* by Martin and McCloskey.

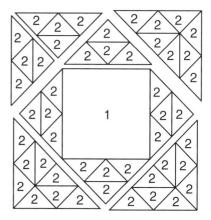

★★ **12" Ocean Waves,**
p. 30

Patch Name	Fin. Size
1. S1	6"
2. T4	3"

Traditional block made by Chris Hulin. These blocks are traditionally made from scraps and set side by side, turning them so that light always touches dark. Update with contemporary fabrics, if you like. You will need 49 blocks set 7 x 7 for a queen-sized quilt.

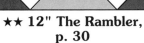

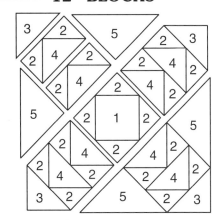

★★ **12" The Rambler,**
p. 30

Patch Name	Fin. Size
1. S1	3"
2. T1	2⅛"
3. T1	3"
4. T4	4¼"
5. T4	6"

Traditional block made by Mary Hazelwood. Set blocks with 3" sashes in the color of the center square. A light 3" square makes a good choice for the setting square. Arrange 36 blocks in 6 rows of 6 for a handsome queen-sized quilt.

★ **12" Virginia Backroads,**
p. 30

Original block designed and made by Judy Martin. Off-center stars are superimposed on Nine-Patch blocks for a new look. Set blocks side by side, turning them as shown at right. For a twin quilt, arrange 35 blocks in 7 rows of 5. For a queen-sized quilt set 49 blocks in 7 rows of 7.

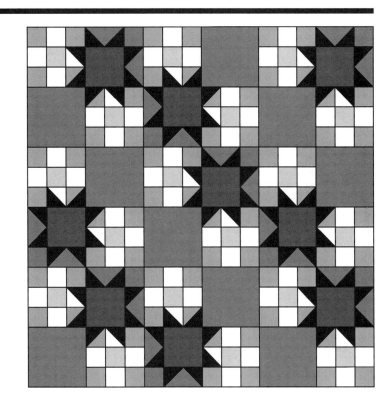

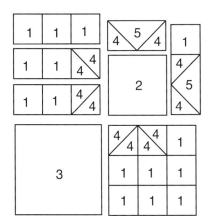

Patch Name	Fin. Size
1. S1	2"
2. S1	4"
3. S1	6"
4. T1	2"
5. T4	4"

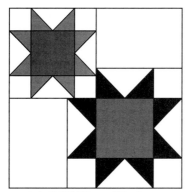

★★ **12" Born Under a Wandering Star, p. 30**

Original block designed and made by Judy Martin. Here is a delightfully simple star block with a new twist: different sized stars! Set blocks side by side as shown at right. Turn them for Log Cabin effects, if you like. A queen-sized quilt takes 49 blocks set 7 by 7.

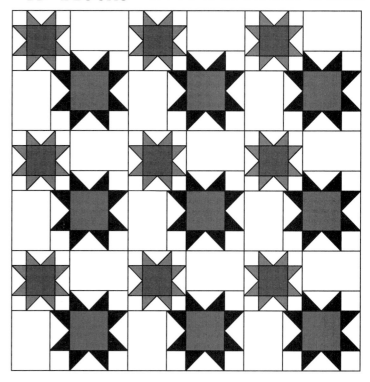

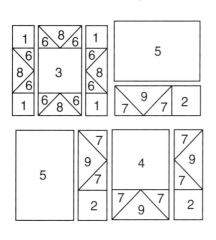

Patch Name	Fin. Size
1. S1	1½"
2. S1	2"
3. S1	3"
4. S1	4"
5. S13	6"
6. T1	1½"
7. T1	2"
8. T4	3"
9. T4	4"

★ **12" Mama's Memories, p. 31**

Patch Name	Fin. Size
1. S1	2"
2. T1	4"
3. T4	4"

Original block designed and made by Judy Martin. Join blocks with 2" light sashes between them. Use scrap setting squares to match the squares in the block. Make a twin quilt from 24 blocks in 6 rows of 4. If desired, add a border of scrappy squares.

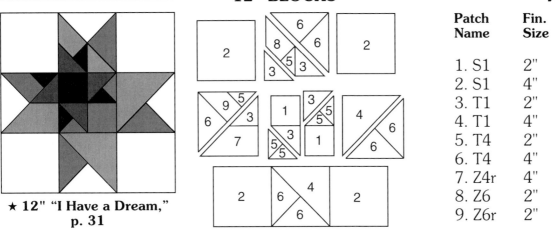

★ 12" "I Have a Dream,"
p. 31

Patch Name	Fin. Size
1. S1	2"
2. S1	4"
3. T1	2"
4. T1	4"
5. T4	2"
6. T4	4"
7. Z4r	4"
8. Z6	2"
9. Z6r	2"

Original block designed and made by Judy Martin. This easy block is one of my favorites. The small, off-center star adds sparkle to a basic star. Arrange blocks with 2" sashes. Cut Z4r and Z6r from unfolded fabric placed face down. 36 blocks in 6 rows of 6 make a queen quilt.

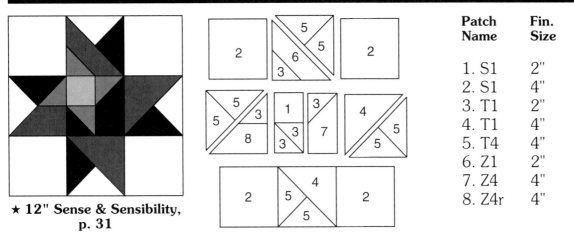

★ 12" Sense & Sensibility,
p. 31

Patch Name	Fin. Size
1. S1	2"
2. S1	4"
3. T1	2"
4. T1	4"
5. T4	4"
6. Z1	2"
7. Z4	4"
8. Z4r	4"

Original block designed and made by Judy Martin. Cut Z4 and Z4r from unfolded fabric, with the Z4r fabric face down. Make a queen-sized quilt from 6 x 6 blocks set with 2" sashes. If you like, incorporate small stars into the border or sashing for a special touch.

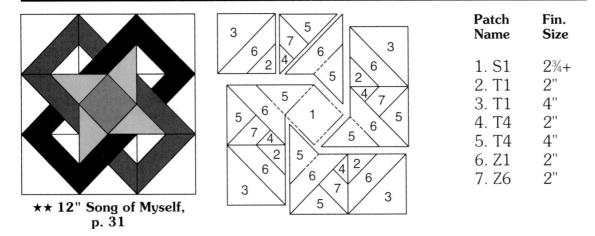

★★ 12" Song of Myself,
p. 31

Patch Name	Fin. Size
1. S1	2¾+
2. T1	2"
3. T1	4"
4. T4	2"
5. T4	4"
6. Z1	2"
7. Z6	2"

Original block designed by Judy Martin; made by Diane Tomlinson. Note the partial seams. Make a twin quilt from 5 x 6 blocks set with 2" sashes. You will need 30 blocks in all.

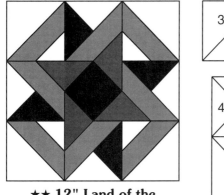
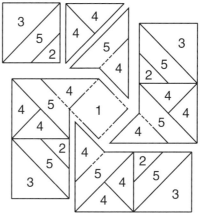

★★ 12" Land of the Midnight Sun, p. 31

Patch Name	Fin. Size
1. S1	2¾+
2. T1	2"
3. T1	4"
4. T4	4"
5. Z1	2"

Original block designed by Judy Martin; reprinted from *Judy Martin's Ultimate Book of Quilt Block Patterns;* made by Lois Rhinehart. Note the partial seams. For a queen-sized quilt, set 49 blocks in 7 rows of 7 with 1½" sashes.

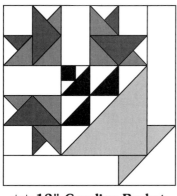
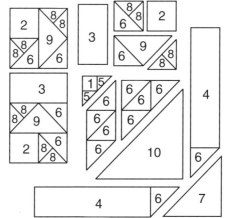

★★ 12" Carolina Basket, p. 31

Patch Name	Fin. Size
1. S1	1"
2. S1	2"
3. S2	4"
4. S4	8"
5. T1	1"
6. T1	2"
7. T1	4"
8. T4	2"
9. T4	4"
10. T4	8½"

Original block designed and made by Judy Martin. Bright flower-colored scraps make this quilt a joy! For a queen-sized quilt, arrange blocks diagonally, 5 across and 5 down. You will need 25 blocks and 16 alternate plain squares. Quilt your favorite fancy motif in the plain squares.

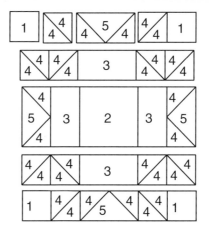

★★ 12" Robbing Peter to Pay Paul, p. 32

Patch Name	Fin. Size
1. S1	2"
2. S1	4"
3. S2	4"
4. T1	2"
5. T4	4"

Traditional block made by Linda Medhus. For a queen-sized quilt, arrange 25 blocks and 24 plain squares alternately in 7 rows of 7. For a twin quilt, you will need 18 blocks and 17 plain squares in 7 rows of 5.

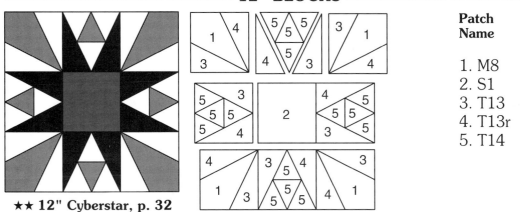

★★ 12" Cyberstar, p. 32

Patch Name	Fin. Size
1. M8	2"
2. S1	4"
3. T13	4"
4. T13r	4"
5. T14	2"

Original block designed and made by Judy Martin. Fold the fabric to cut T13r and T13 at the same time. Set blocks side by side so that four-pointed stars form at the block corners. 35 blocks set 5 x 7 make a striking twin-sized quilt.

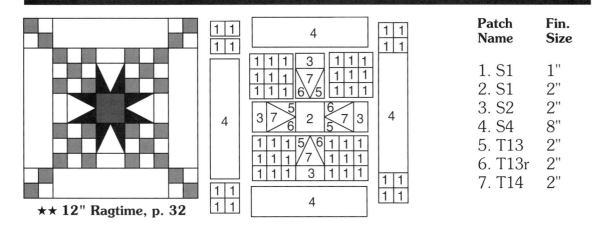

★★ 12" Ragtime, p. 32

Patch Name	Fin. Size
1. S1	1"
2. S1	2"
3. S2	2"
4. S4	8"
5. T13	2"
6. T13r	2"
7. T14	2"

Original block designed by Judy Martin; made by Margy Sieck. Fold the fabric to cut T13r and T13 at the same time. Set blocks with 1" sashes to match the background and 1" setting squares to match the corner squares. For a queen-sized quilt, set 49 blocks in 7 rows of 7.

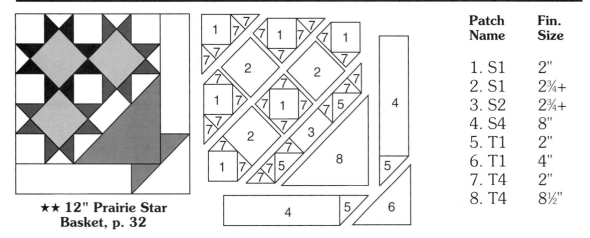

★★ 12" Prairie Star Basket, p. 32

Patch Name	Fin. Size
1. S1	2"
2. S1	2¾+
3. S2	2¾+
4. S4	8"
5. T1	2"
6. T1	4"
7. T4	2"
8. T4	8½"

Original block designed and made by Judy Martin. For a twin quilt, arrange 20 blocks diagonally, point to point, 4 across and 5 down. Place 12 plain squares between blocks, and sew in diagonal rows. Add a pieced border to complete the quilt with a flourish.

★ **12" Costa del Sol,
p. 32**

Original block designed and made by Judy Martin. The blocks can be turned for different sets, Log Cabin fashion, as you can see in the nine-block section at the right. This is especially attractive in scraps. Make a king-sized quilt from 64 blocks in 8 rows of 8.

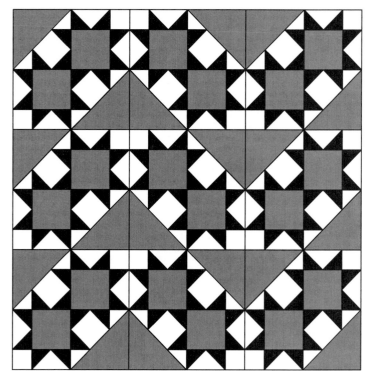

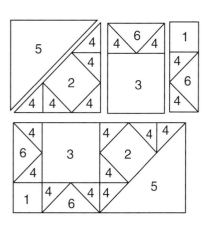

Patch Name	Fin. Size
1. S1	2"
2. S1	2¾+
3. S1	4"
4. T1	2"
5. T1	6"
6. T4	4"

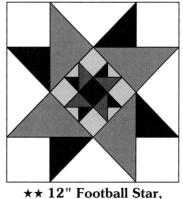

★★ **12" Football Star,
p. 32**

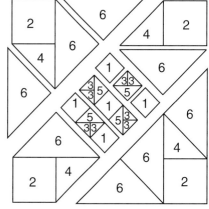

Patch Name	Fin. Size
1. S1	1⅜+
2. S1	3"
3. T1	1"
4. T1	3"
5. T4	2"
6. T4	6"

Original block designed and made by Judy Martin. For a queen-sized quilt, arrange 36 blocks in 6 rows of 6 with 2" sashes between them. For a twin quilt, set 24 blocks in 6 rows of 4 with 2" sashes. For a king-sized quilt or ample queen, set 49 blocks in 7 rows of 7 with 2" sashes.

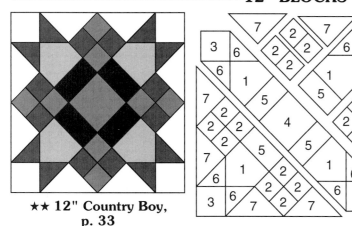

★★ **12" Country Boy,**
p. 33

Patch Name	Fin. Size
1. P9	2¾+
2. S1	1⅜+
3. S1	2"
4. S1	2¾+
5. S2	2¾+
6. T1	2"
7. T4	4"

Original block designed by Judy Martin; reprinted from *Judy Martin's Ultimate Book of Quilt Block Patterns;* made by Margy Sieck. For a queen-sized quilt, arrange 25 blocks and 24 plain squares alternately in 7 rows of 7.

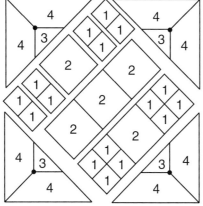

★★ **12" Covered Bridge,**
p. 33

Patch Name	Fin. Size
1. S1	1⅜+
2. S1	2¾+
3. T4	2¾+
4. Z3	6"

Original block designed by Judy Martin; reprinted from *Scraps, Blocks & Quilts;* made by Margy Sieck. Note the four set-in joints. This block looks good in any arrangement. Try setting 25 blocks alternately with 24 plain squares in 7 rows of 7 for a queen-sized quilt.

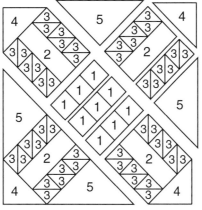

★★ **12" Cross Roads to**
Texas, p. 33

Patch Name	Fin. Size
1. S1	1⅜+
2. S3	4¼"
3. T1	1⅜+
4. T1	3"
5. T4	6"

Traditional block made by Aileen Taylor. For a handsome twin-sized quilt, make 35 blocks and arrange them in 7 rows of 5 with 1½" sashes between them. For a queen-sized quilt, you will need 49 blocks in 7 rows of 7 with 1½" sashes.

★ **12" Sailing by the Stars, p. 33**

Original block designed and made by Judy Martin. Stack light and dark fabric face to face, with the dark face down. This block is stunning in light and dark scraps or in just two fabrics. Set blocks side by side as shown at right. 49 blocks set 7 x 7 make a queen quilt.

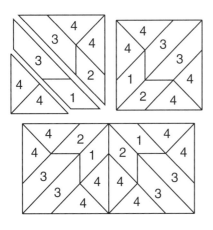

Patch Name	Fin. Size
1. D3	2"
2. D3r	2"
3. Z1	2"
4. T4	4"

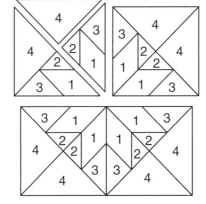

★ **12" Diamond Head, p. 33**

Patch Name	Fin. Size
1. D1	2½"
2. T1	1¾"
3. T4	3½"
4. T4	6"

Original block designed by Judy Martin; made by Chris Hulin. When blocks are set side by side, pinwheels form at the block corners. For a queen-sized quilt, set 49 blocks 7 x 7. For a king-sized quilt, set 64 blocks 8 x 8.

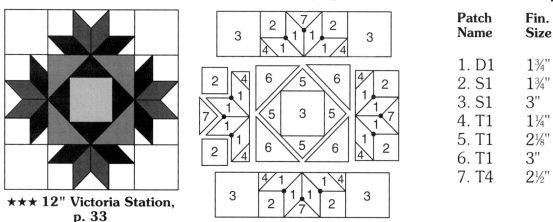

★★★ **12" Victoria Station, p. 33**

Patch Name	Fin. Size
1. D1	1¾"
2. S1	1¾"
3. S1	3"
4. T1	1¼"
5. T1	2⅛"
6. T1	3"
7. T4	2½"

Original block designed and made by Judy Martin. Alternate the blocks with dark plain squares for a striking quilt. You will need 25 blocks and 24 plain squares set in 7 rows of 7 for a queen-sized quilt. Add a simple pieced border for a more generous size. Note the 12 set-in joints.

★★ **12" The River Jordan, p. 34**

Original block designed and made by Judy Martin. Notice the intriguing use of three shades in the star points. Just two basic shapes are needed for this dazzling design! Set blocks side by side as shown at right. For a king-sized quilt, join 64 blocks in 8 rows of 8.

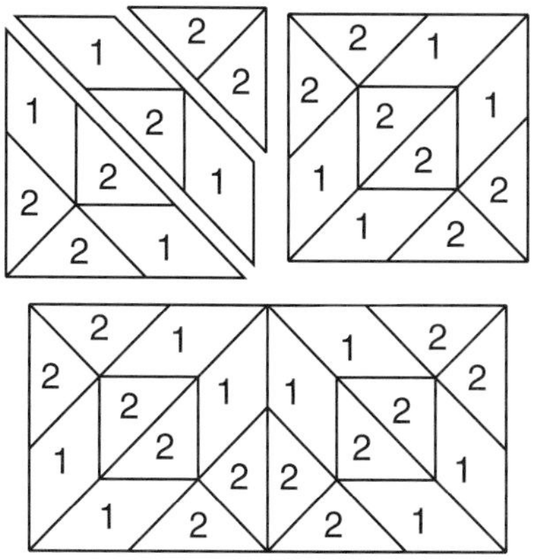

Patch Name	Fin. Size
1. D1	2½"
2. T4	3½"

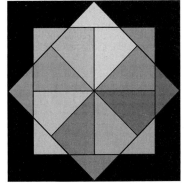

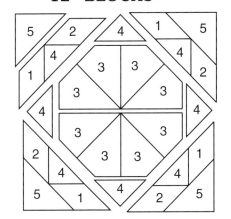

Patch Name	Fin. Size
1. D1	2½"
2. D1r	2½"
3. M9	4¼"
4. T1	2½"
5. T1	3½"

★ 12" Twisting Star, p. 34

Note: For straight grain around the block, D1 and D1r are separate entries. They differ only in grain. Ignore the grain if you wish.

Traditional block made by Judy Martin. Note that D1 differs from D1r only in grain. Place the straight grain on the outside edge of the block. Fold the fabric to cut D1r as you are cutting D1. Set blocks with scrappy 2" sashes. For a twin quilt, make 24 blocks in 6 rows of 4 plus a border.

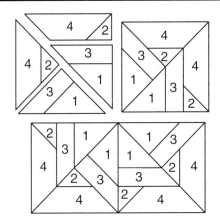

Patch Name	Fin. Size
1. T1	3"
2. T4	2½"
3. Z9	4¼"
4. Z10	6"

★ 12" Tropical Breeze, p. 34

Original block designed and made by Judy Martin. Cut Z9 patches from unfolded fabric, as no reverses are needed. For a special effect, use stripes cut carefully for T4 and Z9. Set blocks with 1¼"-wide sashes to echo the Z9's. For a queen-sized quilt, set 49 blocks in 7 rows of 7.

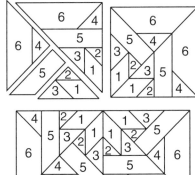

Patch Name	Fin. Size
1. D1	1¾"
2. T1	1¼"
3. T1	1¾"
4. T4	2½"
5. Z9	4¼"
6. Z10	6"

★★ 12" Concord Hymn, p. 34

Original block designed and made by Judy Martin. Cut Z9 patches from unfolded fabric, as no reverses are needed. For a special effect, use stripes cut carefully for T4 and Z9. Set blocks with 1¼"-wide sashes to echo the Z9's. For a queen-sized quilt, set 49 blocks in 7 rows of 7.

★★ 12" Road to Fortune, p. 34

Traditional block made by Margy Sieck. This pattern is great in reproduction prints from the '30s. Cut T9/T9r and Z8/Z8r from folded fabric. Cut T10 from unfolded fabric. Set blocks side by side as shown at right. 35 blocks set 5 x 7 make a queen quilt.

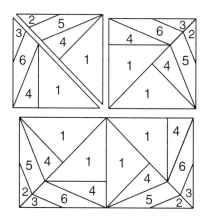

Patch Name	Fin. Size
1. T1	4¼"
2. T9	3"
3. T9r	3"
4. T10	4¼"
5. Z8	3"
6. Z8r	3"

★★ 12" The Silk Road, p. 34

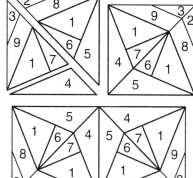

Patch Name	Fin. Size
1. T1	3¼"
2. T9	3"
3. T9r	3"
4. T9	6"
5. T9r	6"
6. T10	3¼"
7. T10r	3¼"
8. Z8	3"
9. Z8r	3"

Original block designed and made by Judy Martin. Cut patches #2-3 and #8-9 from folded fabric. Cut patches #4-7 from medium and dark fabric stacked face to face with the medium face down. Set blocks side by side for a look similar to the Road to Fortune, above.

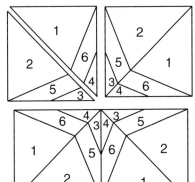

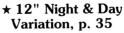

★ **12" Night & Day Variation, p. 35**

Patch Name	Fin. Size
1. T8	6"
2. T8r	6"
3. T9	3"
4. T9r	3"
5. Z8	3"
6. Z8r	3"

Note: For straight grain around the block, T8 and T8r are separate entries. They differ only in grain. Ignore the grain if you wish.

Variation of a traditional block; made by Judy Martin. Place unfolded light and dark fabrics face to face. Cut T9r as you cut T9 with the *dark* fabric face down. Cut T8r as you cut T8 and Z8r as you cut Z8 with the *light* fabric face down.

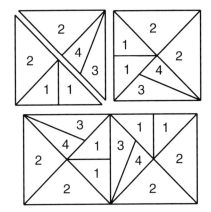

★ **12" Arabian Nights, p. 35**

Patch Name	Fin. Size
1. T4	6"
2. T9	6"
3. T10	4¼"
4. Z9	6"

Or (6" block):
1. T4	3"
2. T9	3"
3. T10	2⅛"
4. Z9	3"

Original block designed and made by Judy Martin. Cut T9, T10, and Z9 patches from unfolded fabric placed face up, as no reverses are needed. For a twin-sized quilt, set 24 blocks in 6 rows of 4 with 2" sashes. For a king size, arrange 49 blocks in 7 rows of 7 with 2" sashes.

★ **12" Olympic Mountain Star, p. 35**

Patch Name	Fin. Size
1. T1	3"
2. T4	6"
3. T9r	6"
4. T10r	4¼"

Original block designed and made by Judy Martin. Cut T9r and T10r from unfolded fabric placed face down, as only reverses are needed. Arrange 25 blocks alternately with 24 light plain squares for a queen quilt. You will need 7 rows of 7. Embellish plain squares with quilting.

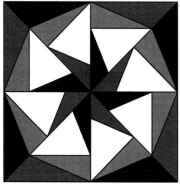

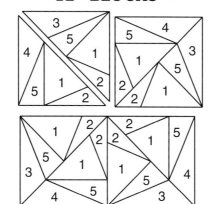

Patch Name	Fin. Size
1. T8	4¼"
2. T9	4¼"
3. T9	6"
4. T9r	6"
5. T10	4¼"

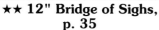

★★ **12" Bridge of Sighs, p. 35**

Original block designed and made by Judy Martin. Cut patches #3 and #4 from two fabrics placed face to face, with the lighter one face down. Cut remaining patches from unfolded fabric, as their reverses are not needed. This design looks wonderful with blocks set side by side.

★★ **12" Vintage Star, p. 35**

Original block designed and made by Judy Martin. Stack light and dark fabric face to face with the dark face down to cut T9 and T9r and other patches. Starbursts form where blocks touch, as you can see at the right. The following block, Aztec Star, is made from the same patches and units, rearranged.

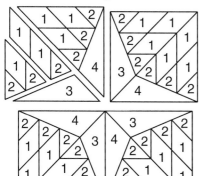

Patch Name	Fin. Size
1. D1	2"
2. T8	2"
3. T9	6"
4. T9r	6"

Note: If desired, cut mirror images in each color of D1 and T8 by turning the fabric stack over for half of them. This will allow you to place the straight grain all around the edges of the block.

★★ 12" Aztec Star, p. 35

Original block designed and made by Judy Martin. See the similar Vintage Star on the previous page for another coloring idea. Stack the two medium fabrics face to face with the darker one face down. You will get the necessary T9r patches as you cut T9's. Set blocks side by side as shown at right. For a queen-sized quilt set 49 blocks 7 x 7.

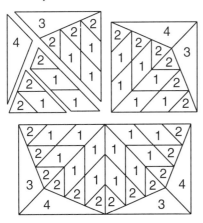

Patch Name	Fin. Size
1. D1	2"
2. T8	2"
3. T9	6"
4. T9r	6"

★★ 12" Palm Sunday, p. 36

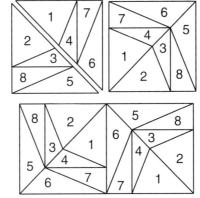

Patch Name	Fin. Size
1. T8	4¼"
2. T8r	4¼"
3. T9	4¼"
4. T9r	4¼"
5. T9	6"
6. T9r	6"
7. T10	4¼"
8. T10r	4¼"

Note: For straight grain around the block, T8 and T8r are separate entries. Ignore the grain if you wish.

Judy's design was inspired by a traditional Palms or Hosanna block; made by Judy Martin. Stack white and light fabrics face to face with the light face down. Stack dark and medium fabrics face to face with the medium face down. Note that T8 and T8r differ only in grain. Place straight grain on the outside of block.

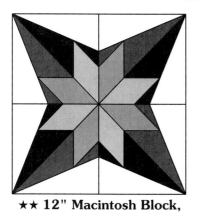

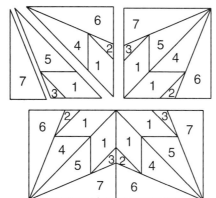

★★ 12" Macintosh Block, p. 36

Patch Name	Fin. Size
1. D1	2½"
2. T9	2½"
3. T9r	2½"
4. T9	6"
5. T9r	6"
6. T10	6"
7. T10r	6"

Original block designed and made by Judy Martin. Stack dark and medium dark fabrics face to face, with the medium dark fabric face down to cut T9r's in both sizes as you cut T9's. Fold fabric to cut T10r's as you cut T10's.

★★ 12" Oliver Twist, p. 36

Original block designed and made by Judy Martin. This is a spin-off from a traditional Virginia Reel. The usual triangles are replaced by graduated pairs of triangles. Coloring in four neighboring hues or values makes blended spirals. Set side by side (see right) for a fantastic quilt. Don't fold the fabric when cutting, as no reverses are needed.

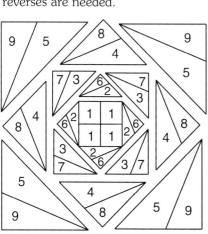

Patch Name	Fin. Size
1. S1	1½"
2. T9	3"
3. T9	4¼"
4. T9	6"
5. T9	8½"
6. T10	2⅛"
7. T10	3"
8. T10	4¼"
9. T10	6"

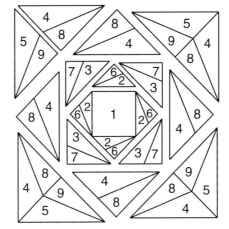

Patch Name	Fin. Size
1. S1	3"
2. T9	3"
3. T9	4¼"
4. T9	6"
5. T9r	6"
6. T10	2⅛"
7. T10	3"
8. T10	4¼"
9. T10r	4¼"

★★ 12" A Red, Red Rose, p. 36

Original block designed and made by Judy Martin. Do not fold the fabric to cut patches. Cut T9r and T10r from face down fabric. Many shades of a similar color accented with touches of green make the rose stand out in this elegant block.

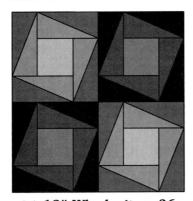

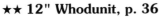

Patch Name	Fin. Size
1. S1	2½"
2. T10	4¼"

★★ 12" Whodunit, p. 36

Original block designed and made by Judy Martin. For a colorful scrap quilt, pair a print with a coordinating solid and a constant center for each quarter. Sew the first rectangle unit to the square with a partial seam. Add the remaining three rectangular units before completing the partial seam.

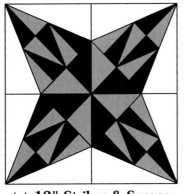

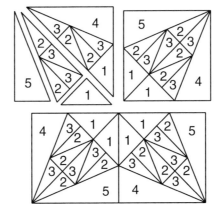

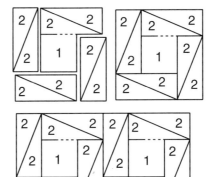

Patch Name	Fin. Size
1. T4	3½"
2. T10	3"
3. T10r	3"
4. T10	6"
5. T10r	6"

★★ 12" Strikes & Spares, p. 36

Original block designed and made by Judy Martin. This was inspired by a traditional Iowa Star block. Cut all patches from folded fabric to yield patches and their reverses. Arrange 25 blocks alternately with 24 light plain squares in 7 rows of 7 for a queen-sized quilt.

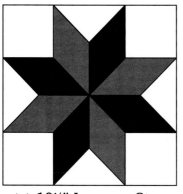

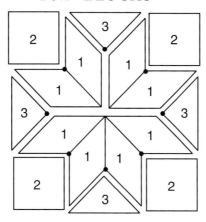

Patch Name	Fin. Size
1. D1	3"
2. S1	3"
3. T4	4¼"

Or (5⅛" block):

1. D1	1½"
2. S1	1½"
3. T4	2⅛"

Or (6" block):

1. D1	1¾"
2. S1	1¾"
3. T4	2½"

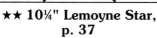

★★ **10¼" Lemoyne Star,**
p. 37

Traditional block made by Judy Martin. This block has just three shapes and sixteen patches. The eight set-ins require accuracy and take a little extra time. This versatile block in one of the smaller sizes at right makes a great accent or pieced border.

★ **10¼" Pinwheel, p. 37**

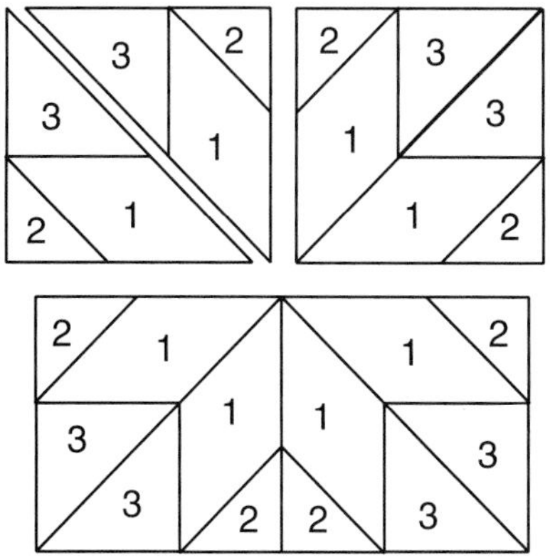

Patch Name	Fin. Size
1. D1	3"
2. T1	2⅛"
3. T1	3"

Traditional block made by Judy Martin. If you prefer, color it like the LeMoyne Star, above. This easy-to-piece block has no set-in seams. Set blocks side by side for a Robbing Peter to Pay Paul effect. Use scraps for a striking queen quilt of 49 blocks set 7 x 7 with a pieced border.

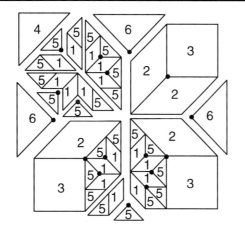

Patch Name	Fin. Size
1. D1	1¼"
2. D1	3"
3. S1	3"
4. T1	3"
5. T4	1¾"
6. T4	4¼"

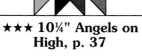

★★★ **10¼" Angels on**
High, p. 37

Original block designed and made by Judy Martin. Sixteen blocks make a terrific wall quilt. Turn the blocks different ways for a lively look. If desired, mix with Lemoyne Star blocks, this page, or Diamonds Are Forever blocks, on the next page. Note the 16 set-in joints per block.

★★★ 10¼" Diamonds Are Forever, p. 37

Original block designed and made by Judy Martin. Set side by side as shown at right, turning as desired. Small stars form at the block junctures. This block mixes well with the LeMoyne Star and Angels on High blocks on page 87. Note the 14 set-in joints.

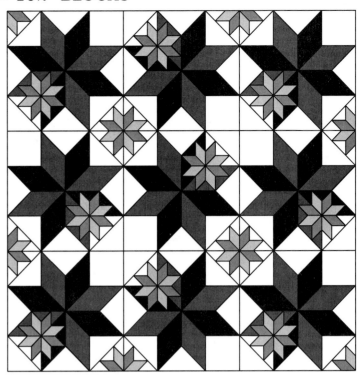

Patch Name	Fin. Size
1. D1	1¼"
2. D1	3"
3. S1	3"
4. T1	3"
5. T4	1¾"
6. T4	4¼"

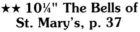

★★ 10¼" The Bells of St. Mary's, p. 37

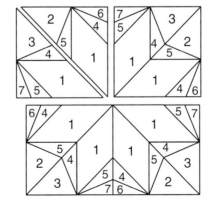

Patch Name	Fin. Size
1. D1	3"
2. T8	3"
3. T8r	3"
4. T9	3"
5. T9r	3"
6. T10	2⅛"
7. T10r	2⅛"

Original block designed by Judy Martin; made by Margy Sieck. Fold the fabric in order to cut reverses at the same time as their counterparts for T8/T8r, T9/T9r, and T10/T10r. Make a queen-sized quilt from 49 blocks arranged in 7 rows of 7 with 2⅛" sashes.

Note: For straight grain around the edges of the units, T8 and T8r are separate entries. They differ only in grain. If you wish to ignore the grain, you may cut T8 for both T8 and T8r.

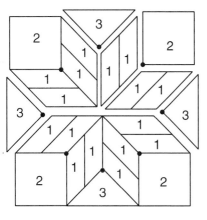

Patch Name	Fin. Size
1. D2	1½"
2. S1	3"
3. T4	4¼"

Note: Cut D2 from unfolded fabric, as no reverses are needed.

★★ 10¼" Liberty Bell, p. 37

Judy's variation of a traditional Liberty block; made by Judy Martin. Consider piecing sashes of two or three strips to match the colors of the star points. Setting squares of four patches complete the design. Make a queen-size quilt from 49 blocks set 7 x 7. Note the 8 set-in joints.

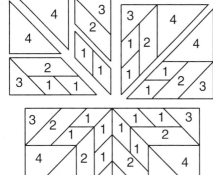

Patch Name	Fin. Size
1. D1	1½"
2. D2	1½"
3. T1	2⅛"
4. T1	3"

Note: Cut D2 from unfolded fabric, as no reverses are needed.

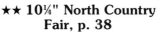

★★ 10¼" North Country Fair, p. 38

Original block designed and made by Judy Martin. For a Robbing Peter to Pay Paul effect, set blocks side by side. Make a twin quilt from 6 x 8 blocks. For another attractive look, make the background all from one striped fabric. Corners will appear to be mitered if you cut carefully.

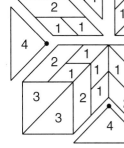

Patch Name	Fin. Size
1. D1	1½"
2. D2	1½"
3. T1	3"
4. T4	4¼"

★★★ 10¼" Niagara Star, p. 38

Original block designed and made by Judy Martin. For background interest, cut patches from one fabric that is variable in color. Set with plain background squares, also variable in color. For a king quilt, 41 blocks alternate with 40 plain squares in 9 rows of 9. Note the 4 set-in joints.

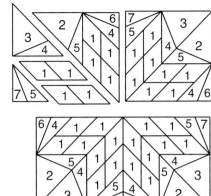

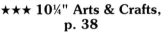

★★★ **10¼" Arts & Crafts, p. 38**

Patch Name	Fin. Size
1. D1	1½"
2. T8	3"
3. T8r	3"
4. T9	3"
5. T9r	3"
6. T10	2⅛"
7. T10r	2⅛"

Note: For straight grain around the block, T8 and T8r are separate entries. They differ only in grain. Ignore the grain if you wish.

Original block designed and made by Judy Martin. Fold the fabric in half to also cut reverses as you cut T8, T9 and T10. T8 and T8r differ only in grain. You can make a queen-sized quilt from 36 blocks set 6 x 6 with 2" sashes and a generous border.

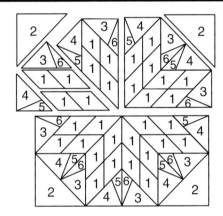

★★★ **10¼" Des Moines Star, p. 38**

Patch Name	Fin. Size
1. D1	1½"
2. T1	3"
3. T8	2⅛"
4. T8r	2⅛"
5. T9	2⅛"
6. T9r	2⅛"

Note: For straight grain around the block, T8 and T8r are separate entries. They differ only in grain. Ignore the grain if you wish.

Original block designed by Judy Martin and made by Chris Hulin. Fold fabric to cut T8r patches as you cut T8 patches. Layer two different unfolded fabrics, the lighter one face up and the darker one face down, to cut T9 and T9r patches respectively.

★★ **10¼" Salsa, p. 38**

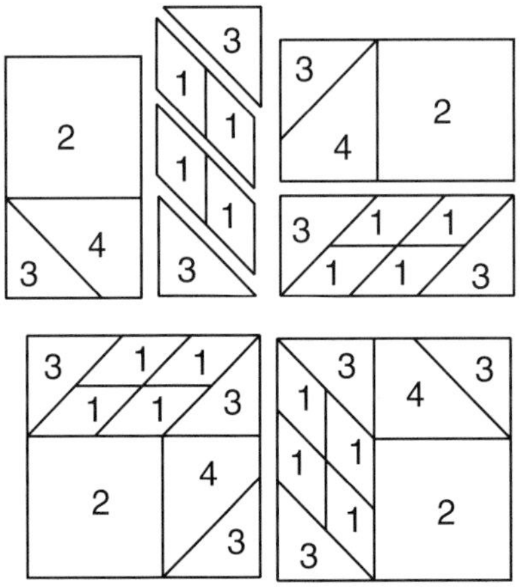

Patch Name	Fin. Size
1. D1	1½"
2. S1	3"
3. T1	2⅛"
4. Z7	3"

Original block designed by Judy Martin; made by Chris Hulin. Cut the Z7 patches from unfolded fabric, as no reverses are needed. Use bright, scrappy sashes and setting squares for an exciting look. Make a twin quilt from 42 blocks arranged in 7 rows of 6 with 2" sashes.

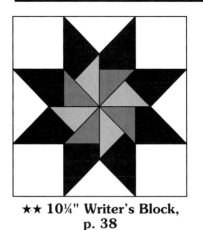

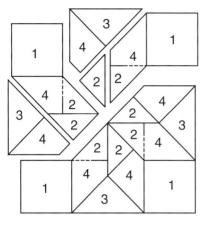

Patch Name	Fin. Size
1. S1	3"
2. T1	2⅛"
3. T4	4¼"
4. Z7	3"

★★ **10¼" Writer's Block, p. 38**

Original block designed and made by Judy Martin. Reprinted from *Judy Martin's Ultimate Book of Quilt Block Patterns*. In each block quarter, sew Z7 to S1. Add T1 with a partial seam, sewing only halfway. After finishing and joining quarters, complete the partial seams.

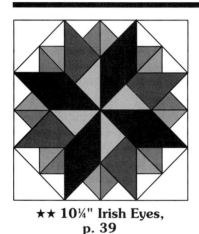

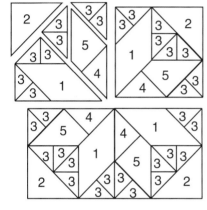

Patch Name	Fin. Size
1. D1	3"
2. T1	3"
3. T4	2⅛"
4. T4	3"
5. Z7	3"

★★ **10¼" Irish Eyes, p. 39**

Original block designed and made by Judy Martin. Use unfolded fabric to cut Z7's, as no reverses are needed. Notice in the photo how neighboring shades create a 3-dimensional effect. 24 blocks set 4 x 6 with 2" sashes and an ample border make a twin-size quilt.

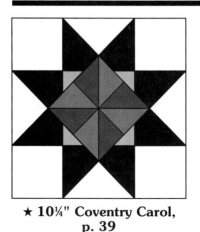

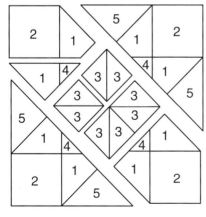

Patch Name	Fin. Size
1. M9	3"
2. S1	3"
3. T1	2⅛"
4. T4	1¾"
5. T4	4¼"

★ **10¼" Coventry Carol, p. 39**

Original block designed and made by Judy Martin. This block makes an easy, beautiful quilt arranged with sashes or a Garden Maze set. Depending on border and sash widths, 36 blocks set 6 x 6 or 49 blocks set 7 x 7 will make a queen-size quilt.

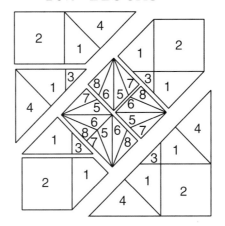

Patch Name	Fin. Size
1. M9	3"
2. S1	3"
3. T4	1¾"
4. T4	4¼"
5. T9	3"
6. T9r	3"
7. T10	2⅛"
8. T10r	2⅛"

★★ 10¼" Song of Solomon, p. 39

Original block designed and made by Judy Martin. Cut T10r reverses as you cut T10 patches from folded fabrics. To cut T9 and T9r place fabrics for them face to face with the darker one face down. For a queen quilt, set 41 blocks alternately with 40 plain squares in 9 rows of 9.

Patch Name	Fin. Size
1. M9	3"
2. S1	4¼"
3. T1	3"
4. T4	1¾"
5. T4	2⅛"

★★ 10¼" Constitution Block, p. 39

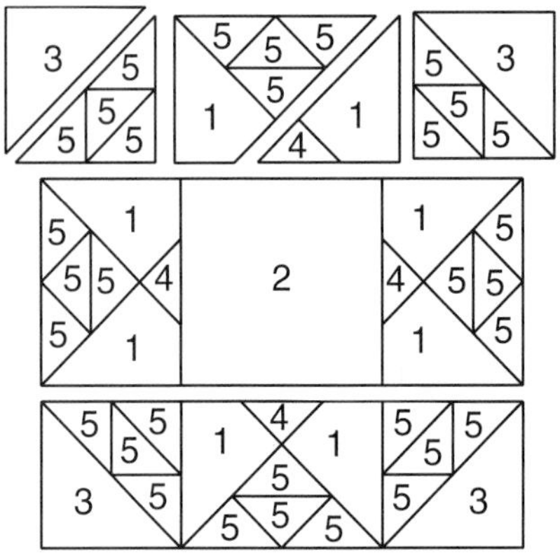

Original block designed and made by Judy Martin. The ring of triangles was inspired by such a ring in Marsha McCloskey's Italian Tile block. A queen-sized quilt requires 36 blocks set 6 x 6 or 49 blocks set 7 x 7, depending on sash and border widths.

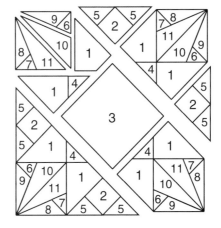

Patch Name	Fin. Size
1. M9	3"
2. S1	1½"
3. S1	4¼"
4. T4	1¾"
5. T4	2⅛"
6. T8	1¼"
7. T8r	1¼"
8. T9	3"
9. T9r	3"
10. T9	4¼"
11. T9r	4¼"

★★ 10¼" St. Joan's Star, p. 39

Original block designed by Judy Martin; made by Diane Tomlinson. Fold fabric to cut reverses as you cut patches #6-9. Note that T8 and T8r are the same shape; only the grain varies. Place the straight grain around the edges of the corner unit. Cut patches #10-11 from two fabrics face to face, with the darker one face down.

Note: See the T8r note on page 90.

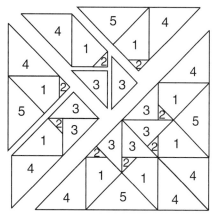

Patch Name	Fin. Size
1. M9	3"
2. T1	⅞"
3. T1	2⅛"
4. T1	3"
5. T4	4¼"

★★ 10¼" Delft Star, p. 39

Original block designed by Judy Martin; made by Margy Sieck. This block was first published in Judy's book, *Scraps, Blocks & Quilts*. It is especially effective with a striped background. For a twin-size quilt, set 35 blocks 5 x 7 with sashes and a border.

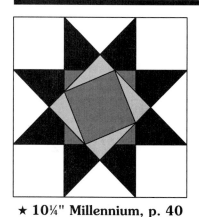

Patch Name	Fin. Size
1. M9	3"
2. S1	3"
3. S1	3¼"
4. T4	1¾"
5. T4	4¼"
6. T10	3"

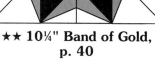

★ 10¼" Millennium, p. 40

Original block designed and made by Judy Martin. Cut T10 from unfolded fabric as no reverses are needed. For an attractive queen-sized quilt, arrange 41 blocks alternately with 40 plain squares in 9 rows of 9.

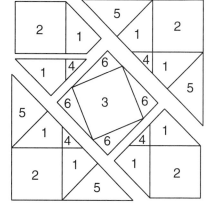

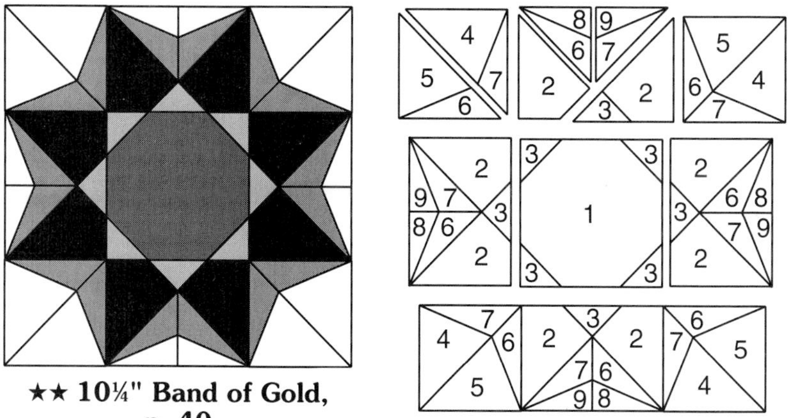

Patch Name	Fin. Size
1. M2	1¾"
2. M9	3"
3. T1	1¼"
4. T8	3"
5. T8r	3"
6. T9	3"
7. T9r	3"
8. T10	2⅛"
9. T10r	2⅛"

★★ 10¼" Band of Gold, p. 40

Original block designed and made by Judy Martin. Fold the fabric to cut reverses as you cut T8, T9, and T10 patches. Thirty-six blocks set 6 x 6 with sashes and a border make a handsome queen-size quilt perfect for newlyweds or Golden Anniversary celebrants.

Note: For straight grain around the block, T8 and T8r are separate entries. They differ only in grain. Ignore the grain if you wish.

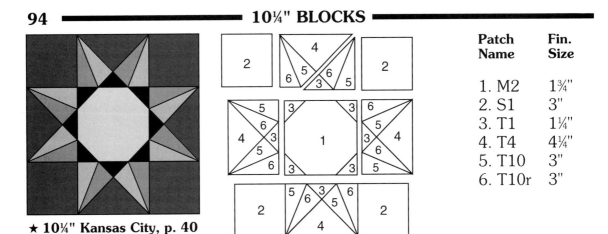

★ **10¼" Kansas City, p. 40**

Patch Name	Fin. Size
1. M2	1¾"
2. S1	3"
3. T1	1¼"
4. T4	4¼"
5. T10	3"
6. T10r	3"

Original block designed by Judy Martin; made by Chris Hulin. Do not fold fabric to cut T10 and T10r. Instead, stack two different unfolded fabrics, the light one face up and the dark face down. This block looks good with sashes. A queen/king quilt can be made from 7 x 7 blocks.

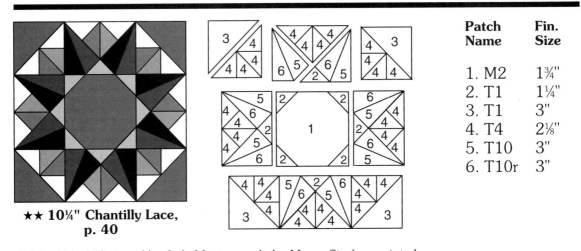

★★ **10¼" Chantilly Lace,
p. 40**

Patch Name	Fin. Size
1. M2	1¾"
2. T1	1¼"
3. T1	3"
4. T4	2⅛"
5. T10	3"
6. T10r	3"

Original block designed by Judy Martin; made by Margy Sieck; reprinted from Judy's *Scraps, Blocks & Quilts.* Cut T10 and T10r patches from face-to-face fabric with the darker fabric face down. Arrange 49 blocks in 7 rows of 7 with 2" sashes between them for a queen-sized quilt.

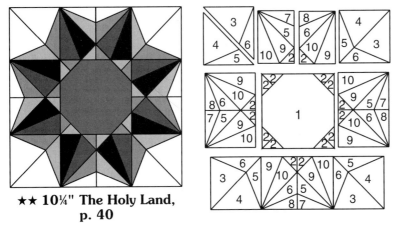

★★ **10¼" The Holy Land,
p. 40**

Patch Name	Fin. Size
1. M2	1¾"
2. T1	⅞"
3. T8	3"
4. T8r	3"
5. T9	3"
6. T9r	3"
7. T10	2⅛"
8. T10r	2⅛"
9. T10	3"
10. T10r	3"

Original block designed and made by Judy Martin. Patch names followed by "r" are reversed. Cut patches #3-8 from folded fabric to yield the reverses as well. Cut patches #9-10 from two different fabrics face to face. The lighter fabric should be face down.

Note: See the T8r note on page 93.

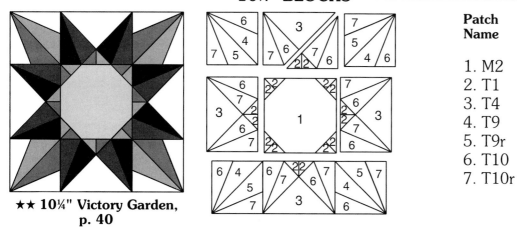

★★ **10¼" Victory Garden,**
p. 40

Patch Name	Fin. Size
1. M2	1¾"
2. T1	⅞"
3. T4	4¼"
4. T9	4¼"
5. T9r	4¼"
6. T10	3"
7. T10r	3"

Original block designed and made by Judy Martin. Fold fabric to cut light background T10r as you cut T10. Place two different fabrics face to face to cut the darker T10 and T10r for the star points. The darkest fabric should be face down.

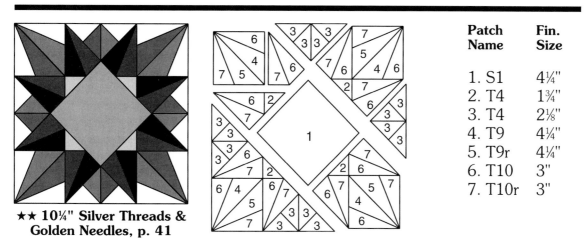

★★ **10¼" Silver Threads &**
Golden Needles, p. 41

Patch Name	Fin. Size
1. S1	4¼"
2. T4	1¾"
3. T4	2⅛"
4. T9	4¼"
5. T9r	4¼"
6. T10	3"
7. T10r	3"

Original block designed and made by Judy Martin. Fold fabric to cut light background T10r as you cut T10. Place two different fabrics face to face to cut the darker T10 and T10r for the star points. The darkest fabric should be face down.

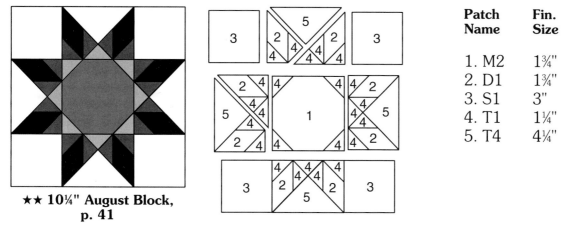

★★ **10¼" August Block,**
p. 41

Patch Name	Fin. Size
1. M2	1¾"
2. D1	1¾"
3. S1	3"
4. T1	1¼"
5. T4	4¼"

Original block designed and made by Judy Martin. This pattern first appeared in *Judy Martin's Ultimate Book of Quilt Block Patterns.* Make a queen-sized quilt from 36 blocks set with sashes and pieced borders. For border ideas, see *Pieced Borders* by Martin and McCloskey.

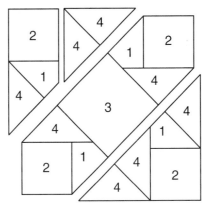

Patch Name	Fin. Size
1. M9	3"
2. S1	3"
3. S1	4¼"
4. T4	4¼"

Or (5⅛" block):

1. M9	1½"
2. S1	1½"
3. S1	2⅛"
4. T4	2⅛"

★ **10¼" Amber Waves, p. 41**

Original block designed and made by Judy Martin. This charming star is even easier than the more usual Evening Star on page 103! Set 6 x 7 blocks with sashes for a twin quilt. Amber Waves makes a perfect accent or border block in the smaller size listed at the right.

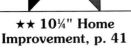

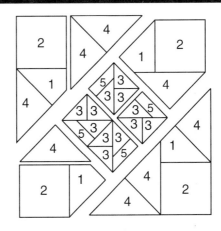

Patch Name	Fin. Size
1. M9	3"
2. S1	3"
3. T4	2⅛"
4. T4	4¼"
5. Z9r	2⅛"

★★ **10¼" Home Improvement, p. 41**

Original block designed and made by Judy Martin. Cut Z9r patches from a single layer of fabric face down, following the directions for Z9 on page 128. Note that no Z9's are needed, just Z9r's.

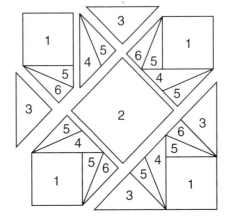

Patch Name	Fin. Size
1. S1	3"
2. S1	4¼"
3. T4	4¼"
4. T9	4¼"
5. T10	3"
6. T10r	3"

★ **10¼" The Night Watch, p. 41**

Original block designed by Judy Martin; made by Diane Tomlinson. Do not fold fabric for T9, T10, and T10r patches. Cut T10r from a single layer of face-down fabric. This may be stacked with the face-up T10 fabric to cut both at the same time, though their quantities vary.

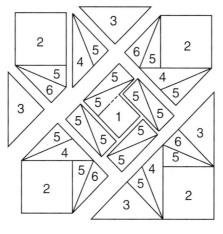

Patch Name	Fin. Size
1. S1	1¾"
2. S1	3"
3. T4	4¼"
4. T9	4¼"
5. T10	3"
6. T10r	3"

★★ 10¼" Graceland, p. 41

Original block designed and made by Judy Martin. Cut T9 and T10 from unfolded fabric that is face up. Cut T10r from unfolded fabric (face down). Set with alternate blocks. A queen/king quilt takes 41 blocks and 40 alternate plain squares in 9 rows of 9. Note the partial seam.

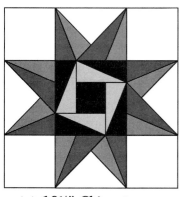

Patch Name	Fin. Size
1. S1	1¾"
2. S1	3"
3. T4	4¼"
4. T9	4¼"
5. T10	3"
6. T10r	3"

★★ 10¼" Chincoteague Mist, p. 42

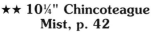

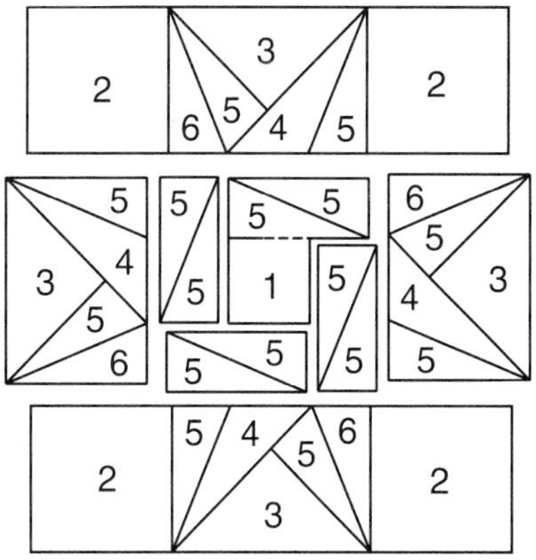

Original block designed by Judy Martin; made by Chris Hulin. This is a variation of Judy's Graceland block, above. Cut T9 and T10 from unfolded fabric that is face up. Cut T10r from unfolded fabric that is face down. A diagonal set is perfect for this. Note the partial seam.

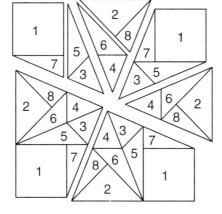

Patch Name	Fin. Size
1. S1	3"
2. T4	4¼"
3. T8	2¼+
4. T8r	2¼+
5. T9	4¼"
6. T9r	4¼"
7. T10	3"
8. T10r	3"

★★ 10¼" A Midsummer Night's Dream, p. 42

Original block designed and made by Judy Martin. Do not fold the fabric for T8, T9, and T10 patches and their reverses. Cut patches with the fabric face up for T8, T9, and T10; face down for their reverses. T8 and T8r have different grains. Place straight grain on edges of units.

Note: For straight grain around the units, T8 and T8r are separate entries. They differ only in grain. Ignore the grain if you wish.

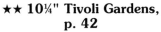

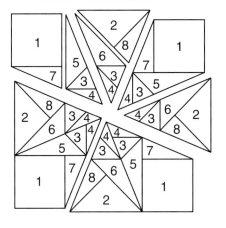

★★ **10¼" Tivoli Gardens,**
p. 42

Patch Name	Fin. Size
1. S1	3"
2. T4	4¼"
3. T8	1¾"
4. T9	2¼+
5. T9	4¼"
6. T9r	4¼"
7. T10	3"
8. T10r	3"

Original block designed and made by Judy Martin. Do not fold fabric to cut patches #3-8. Cut T8, T9, and T10 from fabric that is face up. Cut T9r and T10r from fabric that is face down. You may stack face up and face down fabrics to cut patches and their reverses at one time.

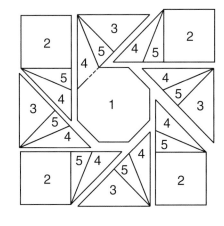

★ **10¼" Jabberwocky,**
p. 42

Patch Name	Fin. Size
1. M2	1¾"
2. S1	3"
3. T4	4¼"
4. T9	4¼"
5. T10	3"

Original block designed and made by Judy Martin. This easy star shines in any style, from country scraps to jaunty brights. After making the eight units shown, attach one to the center with a partial seam, stitching only halfway. Join the other units, then complete the first seam.

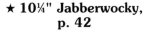

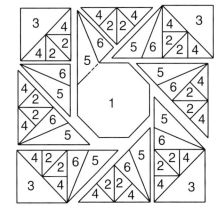

★★ **10¼" Sun & Sea,**
p. 42

Patch Name	Fin. Size
1. M2	1¾"
2. T1	1½"
3. T1	3"
4. T4	2⅛"
5. T9	4¼"
6. T10	3"

Original block designed and made by Judy Martin. Cut T9 and T10 from unfolded fabric, as no reverses are needed. Attach the first of eight units to the octagon with a partial seam, sewing only halfway. Add the other seven units before completing the partial seam.

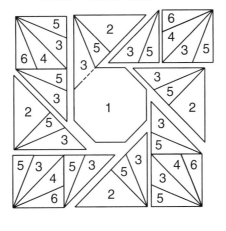

★★ 10¼" Midnight Ride,
p. 42

Patch Name	Fin. Size
1. M2	1¾"
2. T4	4¼"
3. T9	4¼"
4. T9r	4¼"
5. T10	3"
6. T10r	3"

Original block designed by Judy Martin; made by Jane Bazyn. Use unfolded fabrics, with T9 and T10 fabrics face up, T9r and T10r fabrics face down. Attach the first of eight units to the center with a partial seam, sewing halfway. Complete the seam after attaching other units.

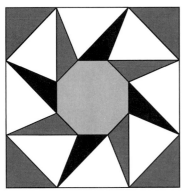

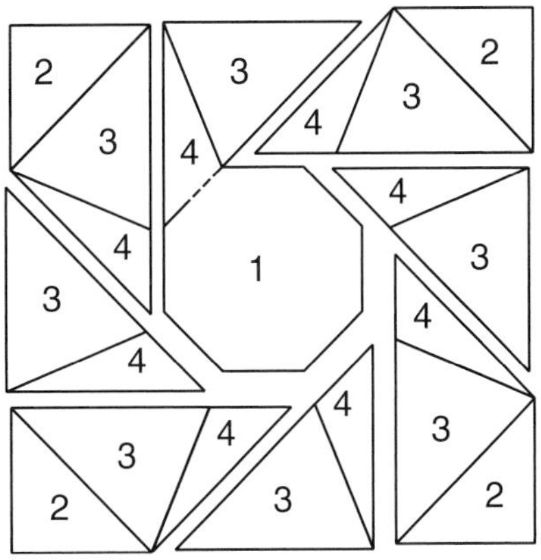

★★ 10¼" Penny Lane,
p. 43

Patch Name	Fin. Size
1. M2	1¾"
2. T1	3"
3. T8r	4¼"
4. T9	4¼"

Note: T8r is listed instead of T8 in order to allow for straight grain around the block. The shape is the same, only the grain differs.

Original block designed and made by Judy Martin. Do not fold the fabric, as you do not need to cut mirror images. Cut the T8r patches from face down fabric following directions for T8 on page 124. The first of the eight units is sewn with a partial seam. Complete it as the last step.

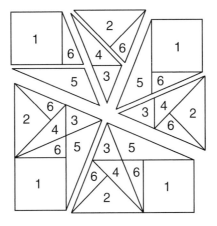

★★ 10¼" Oregon Coast,
p. 43

Patch Name	Fin. Size
1. S1	3"
2. T4	4¼"
3. T8	2¼+
4. T9r	4¼"
5. T9	5½+
6. T10r	3"

Original block designed and made by Judy Martin. Do not fold the fabric, as mirror images are not desired. Cut T9r and T10r from fabric that is face down, following directions for T9 and T10 on page 125. Choose two shades of one color for patches #4-6.

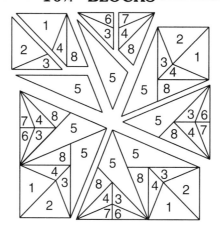

★★ **10¼" National Champion, p. 43**

Patch Name	Fin. Size
1. T8	3"
2. T8r	3"
3. T9	3"
4. T9r	3"
5. T9	5½+
6. T10	2⅛"
7. T10r	2⅛"
8. T10r	3"

Note: For straight grain around the block, T8 and T8r are separate entries. You may ignore the grain if you wish.

Original block designed and made by Judy Martin. Cut patches #5 and #8 from unfolded fabric, face up for T9 and face down for T10r. T8 and T8r differ only in grain. Cut the remaining patches from folded fabric to yield mirror-image pairs.

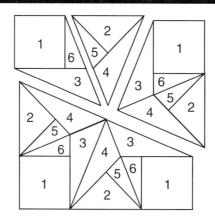

★★ **10¼" Paper of Pins, p. 43**

Patch Name	Fin. Size
1. S1	3"
2. T4	4¼"
3. T9	5½+
4. T9r	5½+
5. T10	3"
6. T10r	3"

Original block designed and made by Judy Martin. Stack medium fabric (face down) and dark fabric (face up) to cut at the same time. Set with sashes or alternate blocks for a lovely quilt. If desired, press open the last three seams to minimize bulk at the block center.

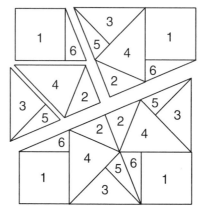

★ **10¼" Bluegrass Block, p. 43**

Patch Name	Fin. Size
1. S1	3"
2. T4	3¼"
3. T4	4¼"
4. T8	4¼"
5. T10	3"
6. T10r	3"

Original block designed and made by Judy Martin. Stack the two medium fabrics, with the darker of the two face down and the lighter one face up, to cut patches and reverses at once. Set 49 blocks with sashes to make a queen-sized quilt having 7 rows of 7 blocks.

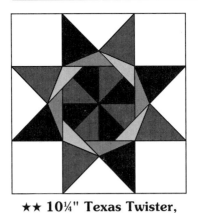

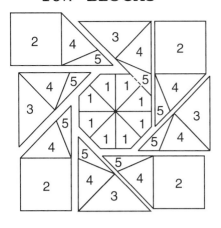

★★ 10¼" Texas Twister, p. 43

Patch Name	Fin. Size
1. M9	2⅛"
2. S1	3"
3. T4	4¼"
4. T8	3"
5. T9	3"

Original block designed and made by Judy Martin. Inspired by Marsha McCloskey's Ringed Star pattern. Use a partial seam to sew the first of the eight units to the block center. Complete the seam after adding the remaining seven units. Cut T9 from unfolded fabric.

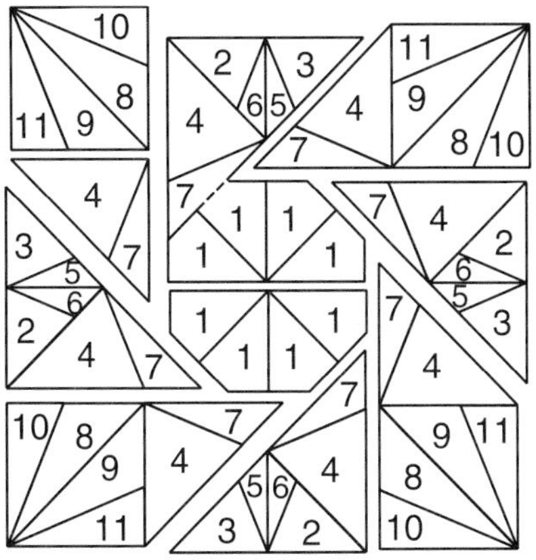

★★★ 10¼" The Rain in Spain, p. 44

Patch Name	Fin. Size
1. M9	2⅛"
2. T8	2⅛"
3. T8r	2⅛"
4. T8	3"
5. T9	2⅛"
6. T9r	2⅛"
7. T9r	3"
8. T9	4¼"
9. T9r	4¼"
10. T10	3"
11. T10r	3"

Note: See T8r note below.

Original block designed by Judy Martin; made by Diane Tomlinson. Related to Judy's Texas Twister, above. Join the first of the eight units to the block center using a partial seam. Finish the seam after adding the remaining seven units. Pay attention to the reverses when cutting.

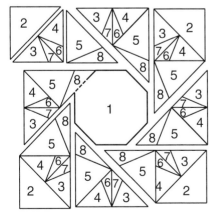

★★★ 10¼" Twist & Shout, p. 44

Patch Name	Fin. Size
1. M2	1¾"
2. T1	3"
3. T8	2⅛"
4. T8r	2⅛"
5. T8	3"
6. T9	2⅛"
7. T9r	2⅛"
8. T9	3"

Note: For straight grain around the block, T8 and T8r are separate entries. You may ignore the grain if you wish.

Original block designed by Judy Martin; made by Jane Bazyn. Join the first of the eight units to the block center using a partial seam. Finish the seam after adding the remaining seven units. #3 and #4 differ only in grain. Cut #5-8 from unfolded fabric, paying attention to "r's." You may stack fabrics for #6 and 7 face to face to cut both T9 and T9r at once.

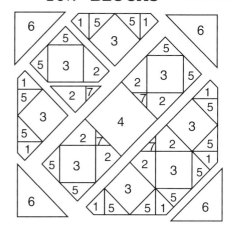

Patch Name	Fin. Size
1. M9	1½"
2. M9	2⅛"
3. S1	2⅛"
4. S1	3"
5. T1	1½"
6. T1	3"
7. T4	1¼"

★★ **10¼" Piccadilly Circus, p. 44**

Original block designed and made by Judy Martin. This block is also the center of the Desert Twilight block on page 17. See the piecing diagram. Note that you do not make diamond-shaped units for the ring surrounding the star and squares. It is easier to sew in rows as shown.

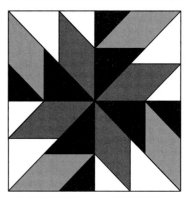

★ **10¼" Diamond Jubilee, p. 44**

Original block designed by Judy Martin; made by Chris Hulin; first published in *Judy Martin's Ultimate Book of Quilt Block Patterns.* Diamond Jubilee is a very easy block that makes an intriguing tessellating pattern of light and dark pinwheels when set side by side, as shown at the right.

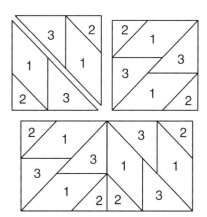

Patch Name	Fin. Size
1. D1	3"
2. T1	2⅛"
3. T1	3"

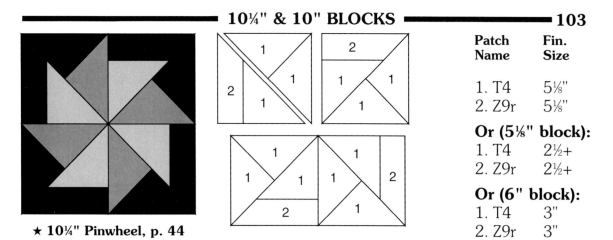

★ **10¼" Pinwheel, p. 44**

Patch Name	Fin. Size
1. T4	5⅛"
2. Z9r	5⅛"

Or (5⅛" block):

1. T4	2½+
2. Z9r	2½+

Or (6" block):

1. T4	3"
2. Z9r	3"

Traditional block made by Judy Martin. This simple block also is a wonderful accent or border block in a smaller size, as described at the right. Note that for all sizes, cut the Z9r patches as described on page 128 for Z9, however, use unfolded fabric that is face down.

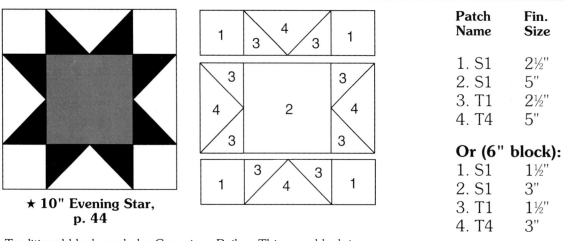

★ **10" Evening Star, p. 44**

Patch Name	Fin. Size
1. S1	2½"
2. S1	5"
3. T1	2½"
4. T4	5"

Or (6" block):

1. S1	1½"
2. S1	3"
3. T1	1½"
4. T4	3"

Traditional block made by Genevieve Bailey. This easy block is a perennial favorite. It is found within many other blocks, incuding several of the Grand blocks on pages 17-25. Use this versatile block in the smaller size at right in pieced borders for a quilt of 12" blocks.

★ **10" Burnham Square Variation, p. 45**

Patch Name	Fin. Size
1. S1	1¼"
2. S1	2½"
3. S4	5"
4. T1	1¼"
5. T1	2½"
6. T4	2½"

The traditional Burnham Square block has three narrower rectangles in the place of the two in Judy's version. Made by Judy Martin. Set blocks with 2½"-wide sashes and setting squares. A secondary pattern of Shooflies forms at the block corners. 35 blocks set 5 x 7 make a twin quilt.

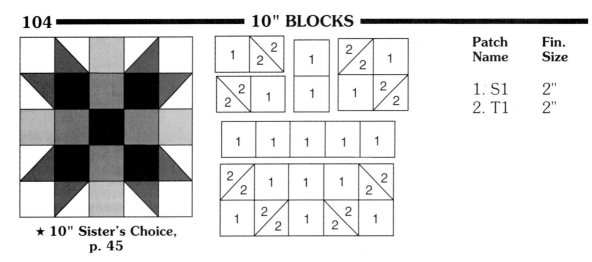

★ 10" Sister's Choice, p. 45

Patch Name	Fin. Size
1. S1	2"
2. T1	2"

Traditional block made by Donna Davis. This simple pattern is lovely in scrap fabrics. For a twin-sized quilt, set 35 blocks 5 x 7 with 2" sashes. For a queen-sized quilt, make 49 blocks. Set them 7 x 7 with 2" sashes.

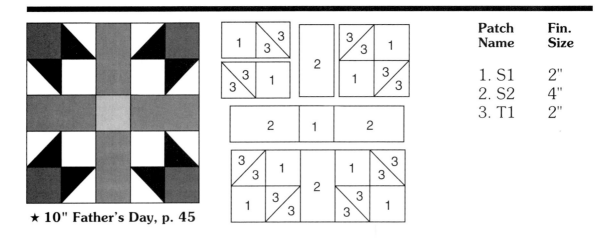

★ 10" Father's Day, p. 45

Patch Name	Fin. Size
1. S1	2"
2. S2	4"
3. T1	2"

Original block designed by Judy Martin; made by Margy Sieck; first published in Judy's *Scraps, Blocks & Quilts.* For a terrific quilt, piece sashes from one dark S3 (6") and two S1 squares to match the block centers. The quilt will look as though blocks cross over the sashes.

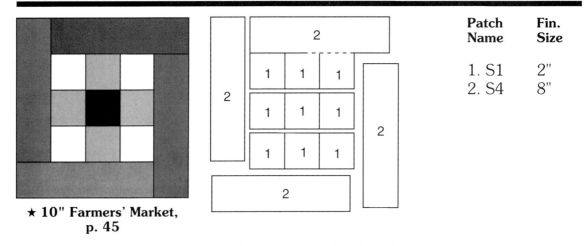

★ 10" Farmers' Market, p. 45

Patch Name	Fin. Size
1. S1	2"
2. S4	8"

Original block designed and made by Judy Martin. Make blocks from scraps and set them side by side for a charming quilt. Note that the first rectangle is sewn to the Nine-Patch center with a partial seam, stitching only halfway. Complete this seam after adding the other rectangles.

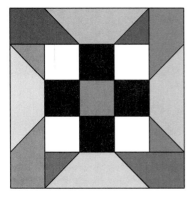

★ **10" Kutztown Puzzle,
p. 45**

Original block designed and made by Judy Martin. Set side by side as shown at right. Stars form at the block junctures. Do not fold fabric to cut Z4's. Use a partial seam to sew the first rectangle unit to the center unit. Complete this seam after adding other units.

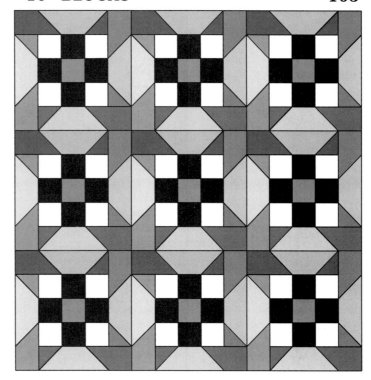

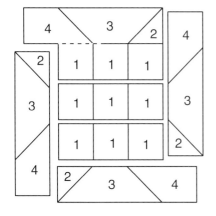

Patch Name	Fin. Size
1. S1	2"
2. T1	2"
3. Z3	6"
4. Z4	4"

★ **10" Cross & Crown,
p. 45**

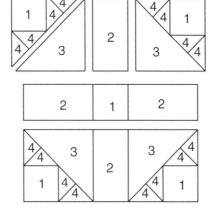

Patch Name	Fin. Size
1. S1	2"
2. S2	4"
3. T1	4"
4. T4	2"

Traditional block made by Dawn Bowman. For a queen-sized quilt, make 36 blocks. Arrange them six across and six down with 25 alternate plain squares in a diagonal set. Finish the quilt with flair with a pieced border. You will find 200 border patterns in *Pieced Borders*.

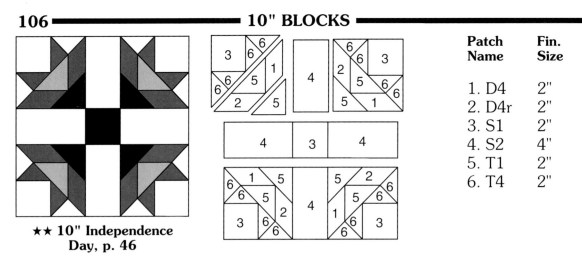

★★ **10" Independence Day, p. 46**

Patch Name	Fin. Size
1. D4	2"
2. D4r	2"
3. S1	2"
4. S2	4"
5. T1	2"
6. T4	2"

Original block designed and made by Judy Martin. Fold the fabric to cut D4 and D4r patches at the same time. Arrange 41 blocks alternately with 40 plain squares in 9 rows of 9 for a queen-sized quilt.

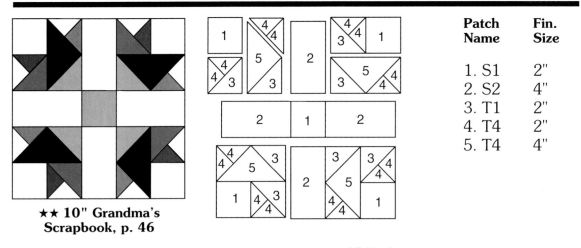

★★ **10" Grandma's Scrapbook, p. 46**

Patch Name	Fin. Size
1. S1	2"
2. S2	4"
3. T1	2"
4. T4	2"
5. T4	4"

Original block designed and made by Judy Martin. Arrange 35 blocks in 7 rows of 5 with 2" sashes between them. This makes a delightfully scrappy twin quilt.

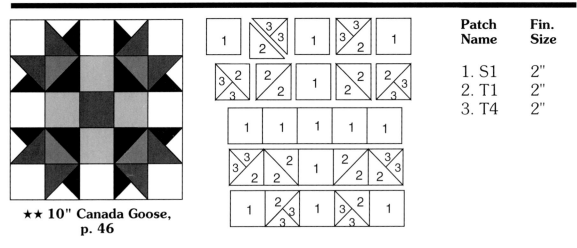

★★ **10" Canada Goose, p. 46**

Patch Name	Fin. Size
1. S1	2"
2. T1	2"
3. T4	2"

Original block designed by Judy Martin; made by Margy Sieck. You will need 32 blocks plus 31 alternate plain squares for a twin-sized quilt. Alternate the blocks and plain squares in 9 rows of 7.

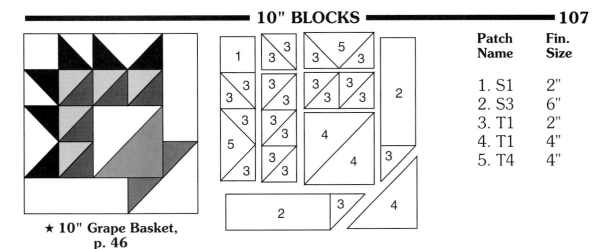

Patch Name	Fin. Size
1. S1	2"
2. S3	6"
3. T1	2"
4. T1	4"
5. T4	4"

★ 10" Grape Basket, p. 46

Traditional block made by Ardis Winters. Try a diagonal set with 2" sashes for an appealing quilt. You will need 25 blocks for a queen-sized quilt or 20 blocks for a twin-sized quilt. Arrange the blocks 4 or 5 in width and 5 in length. Add a border to complete the quilt.

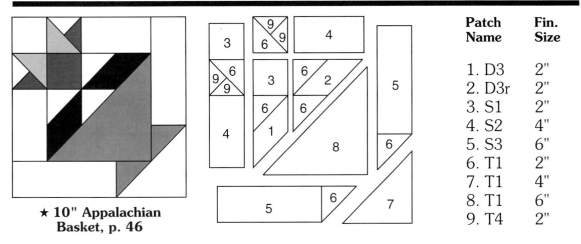

Patch Name	Fin. Size
1. D3	2"
2. D3r	2"
3. S1	2"
4. S2	4"
5. S3	6"
6. T1	2"
7. T1	4"
8. T1	6"
9. T4	2"

★ 10" Appalachian Basket, p. 46

Original block designed and made by Judy Martin. Fold the fabric to cut D3 and D3r at once. This block looks its best set diagonally. For a twin-sized quilt, make 30 blocks. Arrange them five across and six down with 20 alternate plain squares.

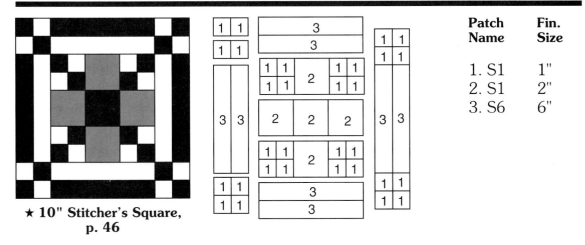

Patch Name	Fin. Size
1. S1	1"
2. S1	2"
3. S6	6"

★ 10" Stitcher's Square, p. 46

Original block designed by Judy Martin; made by Ardis Winters; first published in *Judy Martin's Ultimate Book of Quilt Block Patterns*. This block is made entirely of squares and rectangles for sheer simplicity. Set blocks with sashes and setting squares for a winning design.

★ **10" Elementary Block,
p. 47**

Original block designed and made by Judy Martin. This is particulary attractive made from scraps. Set blocks side by side as shown at right. Make a queen/king-sized quilt from 81 blocks in 9 rows of 9. Make a twin-sized quilt from 63 blocks in 9 rows of 7.

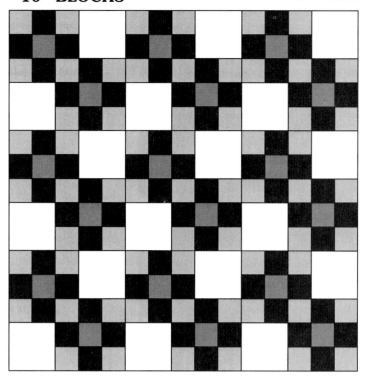

Patch Name	Fin. Size
1. S1	2"
2. S1	4"

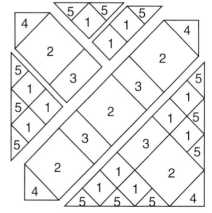

★★ **10" Domino &
Squares, p. 47**

Patch Name	Fin. Size
1. S1	1⅜+
2. S1	2¾+
3. S2	2¾+
4. T1	2"
5. T4	2"

Traditional block made by Margy Sieck. For a handsome queen-sized quilt, set 41 blocks straight with alternate plain squares. Arrange the blocks and squares 9 x 9. You will need 40 plain squares. For a twin-sized quilt, you will need 32 blocks and 31 plain squares arranged 7 x 9.

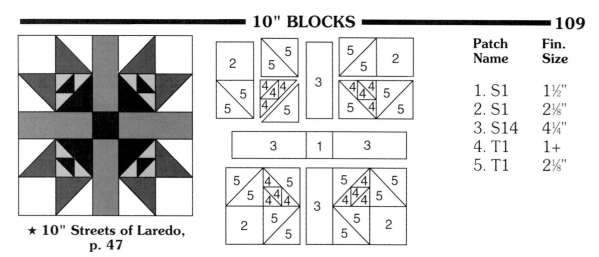

★ 10" Streets of Laredo,
p. 47

Patch Name	Fin. Size
1. S1	1½"
2. S1	2⅛"
3. S14	4¼"
4. T1	1+
5. T1	2⅛"

Original block designed and made by Judy Martin. Set this block with 1½"-wide sashes and setting squares to echo the block center. 48 blocks set 6 x 8 make a twin-sized quilt. For a queen-sized quilt, arrange 64 blocks 8 x 8 with sashes.

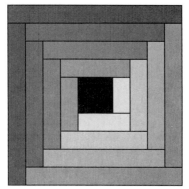

★ 10" Log Cabin, p. 47

Traditional block made by Judy Martin. Sew the #2 patch to #1. Add #3, and so on, in numerical order. Note that there is a light and a dark patch of each patch number except #1, 2, and 10. Log Cabin blocks are traditionally set side by side, with blocks turned to form a pattern. See the quilt section at the right.

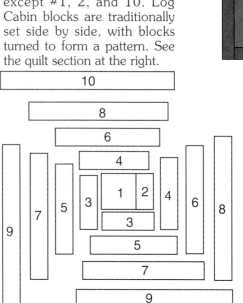

Patch Name	Fin. Size
1. S1	2"
2. S2	2"
3. S3	3"
4. S4	4"
5. S5	5"
6. S6	6"
7. S7	7"
8. S8	8"
9. S9	9"
10. S10	10"

**★★ 10" Great Lakes
Log Cabin, p. 47**

Original block designed and made by Judy Martin. Star blocks are superimposed on Log Cabin blocks for an intriguing design. Each block is made half light and half dark. When blocks are turned in the quilt, different looks are achieved. One look is at right.

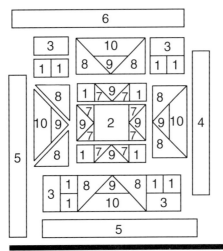

Patch Name	Fin. Size
1. S1	1"
2. S1	2"
3. S2	2"
4. S8	8"
5. S9	9"
6. S10	10"
7. T1	1"
8. T1	2"
9. T4	2"
10. Z11	4"

**★★ 15" Across the Wide
Missouri, p. 47**

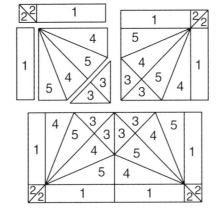

Patch Name	Fin. Size
1. S4	6"
2. T1	1½"
3. T4	3½"
4. T10	6"
5. T10r	6"

Original block designed and made by Judy Martin. To cut, stack light and dark fabric face to face with light face down. You will then be cutting T10r as you cut T10. This block has its own sashes built in. Simply set blocks side by side for an intriguing combination of Pinwheels and Crossed Canoes. 36 blocks (set 6 x 6) make a queen/king quilt.

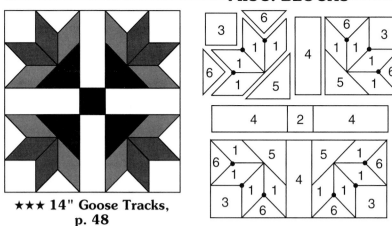

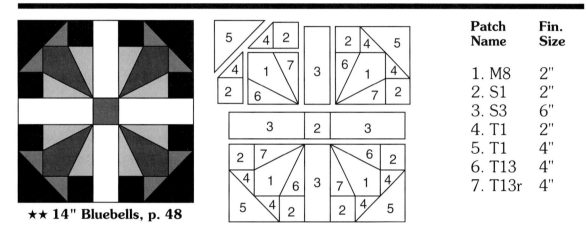

★★★ **14" Goose Tracks, p. 48**

Patch Name	Fin. Size
1. D1	2½"
2. S1	2"
3. S1	2½"
4. S3	6"
5. T1	3½"
6. T4	3½"

Traditional block made by Judy Martin. Note the 12 set-in joints in this block. Set 36 blocks in 6 rows of 6 with 2" sashes for a terrific king-sized quilt. For a twin-sized quilt, set 20 blocks in 5 rows of 4 with 2" sashes and a border.

★★ **14" Bluebells, p. 48**

Patch Name	Fin. Size
1. M8	2"
2. S1	2"
3. S3	6"
4. T1	2"
5. T1	4"
6. T13	4"
7. T13r	4"

Original block designed by Judy Martin; made by Margy Sieck; reprinted from Judy's *Patchworkbook*. Fold the fabric to cut T13r as you cut T13. For a king-sized quilt, arrange 25 blocks alternately with 24 plain squares to make 7 rows of 7.

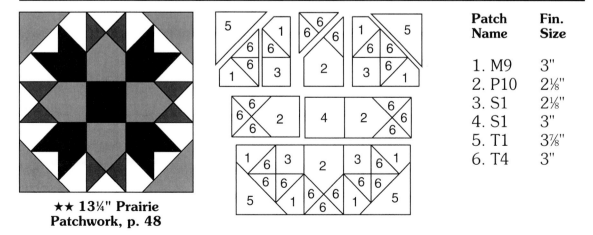

★★ **13¼" Prairie Patchwork, p. 48**

Patch Name	Fin. Size
1. M9	3"
2. P10	2⅛"
3. S1	2⅛"
4. S1	3"
5. T1	3⅞"
6. T4	3"

Original block designed and made by Judy Martin. Judy first published this block in an article she wrote for *Quilter's Newsletter Magazine* in 1993. Set 25 blocks 5 x 5 with 3" sashes and a generous border for a queen-sized quilt.

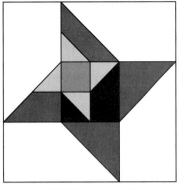
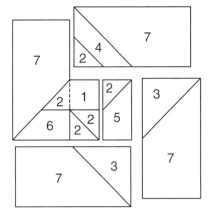

★ **9" Measure for Measure, p. 48**

Patch Name	Fin. Size
1. S1	1½"
2. T1	1½"
3. T1	3"
4. Z1	1½"
5. Z4	3"
6. Z4r	3"
7. Z4	6"

Original block designed by Judy Martin; made by Viola Armstrong. Note the partial seam. Use unfolded fabrics to cut #5-7, with the fabric face up for Z4's and face down for Z4r. Join the first rectangular unit to the square center with a partial seam. Complete this seam as the last step.

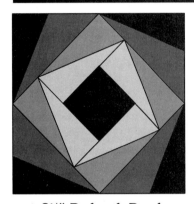
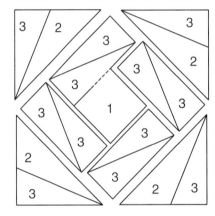

★ **8½" Paducah Puzzle, p. 48**

Patch Name	Fin. Size
1. S1	2½"
2. T9	6"
3. T10	4¼"

Original block designed and made by Judy Martin. Cut patches T9 and T10 from unfolded fabric, as no reverses are needed. Sew the first rectangular unit to the center square only halfway, with a partial seam. Add the 3 remaining units before completing the partial seam.

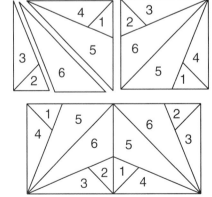

★ **8½" Sydney Star, p. 48**

Patch Name	Fin. Size
1. T8	1¾"
2. T8r	1¾"
3. T9	4¼"
4. T9r	4¼"
5. T9	6"
6. T9r	6"

Note: For straight grain around the units, T8 and T8r are separate entries. They differ only in grain. Ignore the grain if you wish.

Original block designed and made by Judy Martin. Inspired by a traditional Star block. Fold darkest fabric to cut T9r as you cut T9. Place remaining fabrics in face-to-face pairs for cutting, with lighter T8 fabric and the lighter T9 fabric face down.

Queen/King Sampler of 10¼" Blocks (97¾" x 97¾")

Yardage:

8 yards light for backgrounds of blocks
  and plain and pieced borders
¾ yard dark for border triangles
4–5 yards (total) of various fabrics
  for stars and other block patches
9 yards for lining
⅞ yard for binding
Batting to measure 102" x 102"

Cutting:

Light Background fabric:

2 border strips 8¼+" x 76⅞"
  (cut 8¾+" x 77⅜" or longer)
2 border strips 8¼+" x 93½"
  (cut 8¾+" x 94" or longer)

168 T1 (2⅛") for pieced borders
4 T4 (4¼") for pieced borders
4 S1 (2⅛") for pieced borders
63 S1 (5⅛") for Unit 1's
72 T4 (2⅛") for 5⅛" blocks
72 S1 (1½") for 5⅛" blocks
Background patches for 10¼" blocks

Dark fabric:

176 T1 (2⅛") for pieced borders

Various fabrics:

72 M9 (1½") for 5⅛" blocks
72 T4 (2⅛") for 5⅛" blocks
18 S1 (2⅛") for 5⅛" blocks
Patches for desired 10¼" blocks

(Sizes listed are finished sizes.)

Piecing Instructions:

1. Make 36 blocks, each finishing 10¼". Choose from the many presented in *The Block Book.* You may want to change coloring for a consistent background throughout the sampler quilt.

2. Make 18 Amber Waves blocks from page 96 in the 5⅛" finished size. Continue to use the consistent background, if desired.

3. Join four 10¼" blocks, two 5⅛" blocks, and seven 5⅛" (finished) plain squares as shown in the Unit 1 diagram. Make the partial seam as follows: After making four rectangular segments, join the first to the center square with a partial seam, sewing from the aligned edge only halfway down the seamline. Leave the rest of this seam unsewn until you have added the remaining three rectangular segments. Finish the partial seam to complete Unit 1. Make 9 Unit 1's.

4. Keep all of the Unit 1's turned the same way. Join three Unit 1's to make a row. Make three rows like this. Join the rows to complete the quilt center.

5. Sew plain 76⅞"-long (finished) border strips to the sides of the quilt center. Sew plain 93½"-long (finished) border strips to the top and bottom of the quilt center.

6. Use light and dark 2⅛" (finished) T1 triangles to make 168 Unit 2's for the pieced borders. Make four Unit 3's for border centers, using dark 2⅛" T1 triangles and light 4¼" (finished) T4 triangles. Join 21 Unit 2's for half a border strip. Join 21 more facing the opposite direction for the other half. Join the two halves with a Unit 3 between them to complete a border strip. Make four pieced border strips. To two of them, add a 2⅛" (finished) square to each end. These will be for the top and bottom of the quilt.

7. Attach pieced side borders first. Then attach the top and bottom borders to complete the quilt top.

8. Make the lining from three pieces cut 34½" x 102". Quilt as desired. Bind the quilt's edges. Sign and date the quilt as a perfect finishing touch.

Unit 2

Unit 2 Pcg.

Unit 3

Unit 3 Pcg.

Unit 1

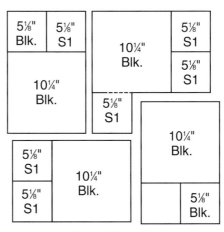

Unit 1 Piecing

Twin Sampler of 12" Blocks (68" x 98")

Yardage:

6 yards light for backgrounds of blocks
   and plain and pieced borders
⅝ yard for dark border triangles
3–4 yards (total) of various fabrics
   for stars & other elements

(excluding the background)
in 6" Judy's Star blocks and the
   12" blocks of your choice
6 yards for lining
¾ yard for binding
Batting to measure 72" x 102"

Cutting: *(Note that all listed sizes are finished sizes.)*

Background fabric:
2 border strips 2" x 90"
   (cut 2½" x 90½" or more)
2 border strips 2" x 64"
   (cut 2½" x 64½" or more)
160 T1 (2") for pieced borders
2 S1 (2") for pieced borders
42 S1 (6") for Unit 1's
48 T4 (3") for 6" blocks
48 S1 (1½") for 6" blocks
Background patches for 12" blocks

Dark fabric:
160 T1 (2") for pieced borders

Various fabrics:
48 T1 (1½") for 6" blocks
48 T4 (3") for 6" blocks
12 S1 (2⅛") for 6" blocks
Patches as needed for the 12" blocks
   of your choice

Piecing Instructions:

1. Make 24 blocks, each finishing 12". Choose from the many presented in *The Block Book.* You may want to change coloring for a consistent background throughout the sampler quilt.

2. Make 12 Judy's Star blocks from page 62 in the 6" finished size. Continue to use the consistent background, if desired.

3. Join four 12" blocks, two 6" blocks, and seven 6" (finished) plain squares as shown in the Unit 1 diagram. Make the partial seam as follows: After making four rectangular segments, join the first to the center square with a partial seam, sewing from the aligned edge only halfway down the side of the square. Leave the rest of this seam unsewn. After adding the remaining three rectangular segments, finish the partial seam to complete Unit 1. Make 6 Unit 1's.

4. Keeping all of the Unit 1's turned the same way, join two Unit 1's to make a row. Make three rows. Join rows.

5. Sew plain 90"-long (finished) border strips to the sides of the quilt center. Sew plain 64"-long (finished) border strips to the top and bottom of the quilt.

6. Use light and dark 2" (finished) T1 triangles to make 160 Unit 2's for the pieced borders. Join 47 Unit 2's all facing the same direction for a side border. Repeat for a second side border. Join 33 Unit 2's, this time all facing the opposite direction, for the top border. Add a 2" (finished) square to one end to complete the top border. Repeat for the bottom border.

7. Attach pieced side borders, then top and bottom borders.

8. Make the lining from two pieces cut 36¼" x 102". Quilt as desired. Bind the quilt's edges. Sign and date the quilt as a perfect finishing touch.

Unit 1

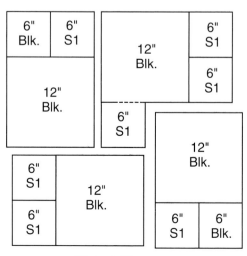

Unit 1 Piecing

Unit 2

Unit 2 Piecing

Please read this before cutting.

The cutting directions in this book may be different from some you have seen. The blocks in *The Block Book* look fresh and exciting in part because they use some shapes that may be new to your rotary cutting repertoire. If you are learning to cut a new shape, cut a strip and a sample patch and check it against the appropriate template on pages 125-142. When you are sure you are cutting correctly, proceed with the rest of the patches.

Rotary Cutting Charts & Illustrations

The rotary cutting information in *The Block Book* comes directly from my book, *Judy Martin's Ultimate Rotary Cutting Reference*. Some sizes have been deleted and others added to suit the blocks in this book. Patch names correspond to those in the *Rotary Reference,* and you will find additional cutting details and yardage figures for these patches there. You will also find a bigger variety of methods and tools to choose from than I had space for here.

To use the cutting charts, find the chart matching your patch name. Find the finished size for your block in the first column of the appropriate cutting chart. Follow that line to the right to find dimensions for cutting the strip and subcuts. The notations in bold at the heads of the columns correspond to the cutting illustrations on the same page.

Every step of cutting the patch is shown. Generally, you cut a strip first. Next you cut off one end of the strip to square it up or to match the angle listed. *Then you cut, laying the rule line listed for your patch on the short end of the strip and cut along the edge of the ruler to make a square, rectangle, diamond or parallelogram.* For some patches, you will need to cut the resulting shape in half diagonally, cut it in quarters, or trim off one or more corners to complete the desired patch.

Some patches are most easily cut with the help of my Shapemaker 45 (S45) tool. Ask for it at your local shop or see page 143 for more information.

Patch sizes followed by a "+" are most readily cut using my Rotaruler 16 (R16). They can also be cut using a regular ruler, estimating halfway between the listed number and the next higher ⅛" on your regular ruler.

Trim Points for Easy Sewing

I strongly recommend trimming points before piecing to help you align the patches perfectly. My Point Trimmer will help you trim points of any 45° angle, such as common triangles, diamonds, and trapezoids. To trim other points, I recommend tracing the templates, and placing two paper patches as if you were going to sew them, with the ends of the seamlines aligned. For each paper patch, draw a line where the other patch crosses the extended point. Trim on the line. You may tape this to the unprinted side of your rotary ruler to use as a trimming guide, if you like.

Full-Size Patterns

Pattern pieces are labeled to match the patch list, with the finished size as well as a patch name. Be sure to look for the *size* as well as the name. These are in alphabetical order. To conserve space, I put smaller templates over larger ones. Include the outer edge of the small template as part of the large one.

Note that a very few templates of the most basic shapes were too large to fit the page. For these, refer to the rotary cutting charts or make a template from the small sketch given.

#D1 DIAMONDS

Cut strip width.

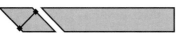

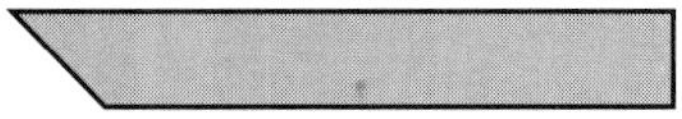

Cut off end at a 45° angle.

Subcut a diamond parallel to the angled end.

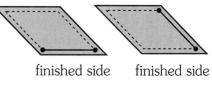

Continue cutting this way.

> Note: "+" means add ¹⁄₁₆" to listed number.

#D1 DIAMONDS

Size	Cutting		
fin. side	cut strip width	cut angle 45°	cut dia- mond
1¼"	1⅜"		1⅜"
1½"	1½+		1½+
1¾"	1¾"		1¾"
2"	1⅞+		1⅞+
2⅛"	2"		2"
2½"	2¼"		2¼"
3"	2⅝"		2⅝"

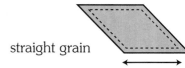

finished side   finished side

straight grain

#D2-D4 PARALLELOGRAMS

Cut strip width.

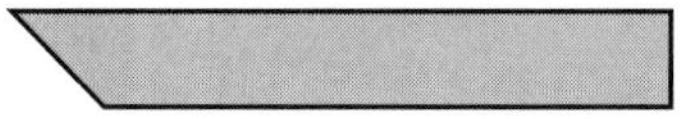

Cut off end at a 45° angle.

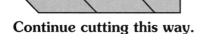

Subcut a parallelogram.

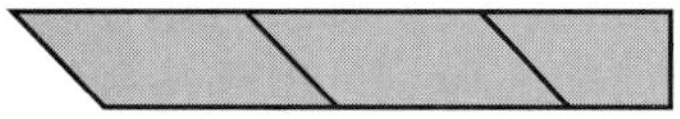

Continue cutting this way.

> Note: "+" means add ¹⁄₁₆" to listed number.

#D2-D4 PARALLELOGRAMS

Size	Cutting		
fin. side	cut strip width	cut angle 45°	cut paral- lelo- gram
D2 1½"	1½+		2⅝"
D3 1½"	2"		1½+
2"	2½"		1⅞+
D4 2"	1½"		1⅞+
3"	2"		2⅝"

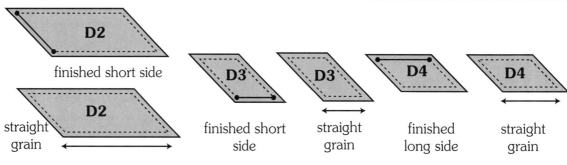

D2 — finished short side

D2 — straight grain

D3 — finished short side

D3 — straight grain

D4 — finished long side

D4 — straight grain

#M2 OCTAGONS

Size	Cutting			
fin. side	cut strip width	cut square	cut dist. from diag.	cut dist. from side
1¾"	4¾"	4¾"	2⅜"	4¾"

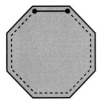 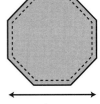

finished side   straight grain

#M2 OCTAGONS

#M2 OCTAGONS

Cut strip width.

Subcut a square.

Cut parallel to the diagonal on 2 adjacent sides, leaving first corner in place as you cut the second corner.

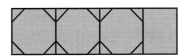

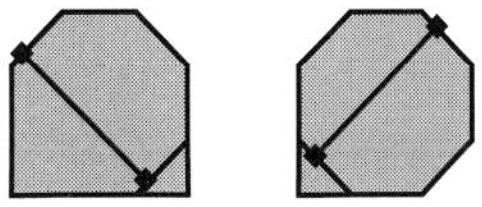

Cut parallel to angled sides to complete octagon.

Continue cutting this way.

#M8 90° KITES

Size	Cutting		
fin. short side	cut strip width	cut square	trim 2 corners*
1½"	3¾+	3¾+	
2"	4¾+	4¾+	

Note: "+" means add ¹⁄₁₆" to listed number.

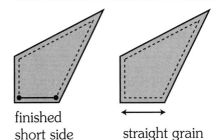

finished short side   straight grain

*Trace the angle from the T13 template on page 141 and tape it to the unprinted side of your rotary ruler to use as an angle guide for trimming off the corners of M8.

#M8 90° KITES

#M8 90° KITES

Cut strip width.

Subcut a square.

F. Cut off 2 corners at 2:1 angles*.

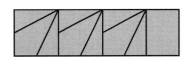

Continue cutting this way.

#M9 135° KITES

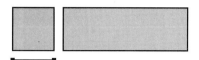

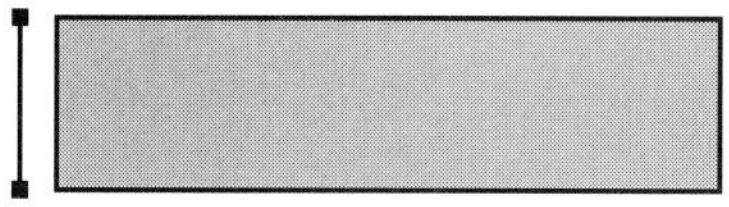

Cut strip width.

Subcut a square.

Cut in half diagonally.

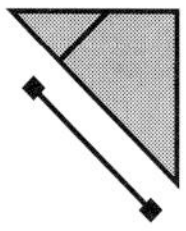

Cut at right angle to long side.

Continue cutting this way.

#M9 135° KITES

Size	Cutting			
fin. long side	cut strip width	cut square	cut in half diagonally	cut long side
1¼"	2⅛"	2⅛"		2⅛"
1½"	2⅜"	2⅜"		2⅜"
1¾"	2⅝"	2⅝"		2⅝"
2⅛"	3"	3"		3"
3"	3⅞"	3⅞"		3⅞"
4¼"	5⅛"	5⅛"		5⅛"
6"	6⅞"	6⅞"		6⅞"

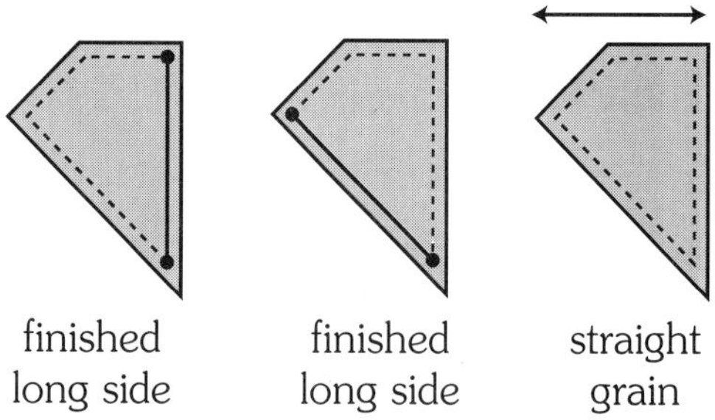

finished long side   finished long side   straight grain

#P6-P10 HALF PRISMS

Cut strip width.

Note: "+" means add ¹⁄₁₆" to listed number.

Subcut a rectangle.

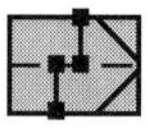

Trim 2 triangles from one end using the S45*.

Continue cutting as shown.

*The short line near the Shapemaker 45's 90° angle should be on the right edge of the rectangle. Center the S45, using the midline-to-side listing. Cut off the two extending corners of the patch. If you don't have an S45, trace the template and tape it to your ruler as a guide.

#P6, P9 & P10 HALF PRISMS

Size	Cutting		
fin. side	cut strip width	cut rec-tangle	mid-line to side
P6			
3"	3½"	5"	1¾"
P9			
2¾+	3¼+	3¼+	1¾(-)*
4"	4½"	4½"	2¼"
4¼"	4¾"	4¾"	2⅜"
P10			
2⅛"	3½"	4⅛"	1¾"

*1¾(-) is slightly smaller than 1¾", by eye

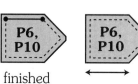
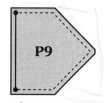
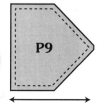

P6, P10 finished side   P6, P10 straight grain   P9 finished long side   P9 straight grain

#S1 SQUARES

Size	Cutting	
fin. side	cut strip width	cut square
1"	1½"	1½"
1+	1½+	1½+
1¼"	1¾"	1¾"
1⅜+	1⅞+	1⅞+
1½"	2"	2"
1¾"	2¼"	2¼"
2"	2½"	2½"
2⅛"	2⅝"	2⅝"
2½"	3"	3"
2¾+	3¼+	3¼+
3"	3½"	3½"
3¼"	3¾"	3¾"
4"	4½"	4½"
4¼"	4¾"	4¾"
4½"	5"	5"
5"	5½"	5½"
5⅛"	5⅝"	5⅝"
6"	6½"	6½"
6⅜"	6⅞"	6⅞"
9⅜"	9⅞"	9⅞"

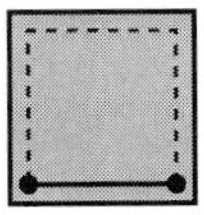

Note: "+" means add ¹⁄₁₆" to listed number.

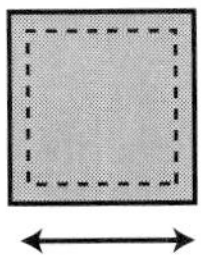

#S1 SQUARES

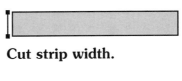

Cut strip width.

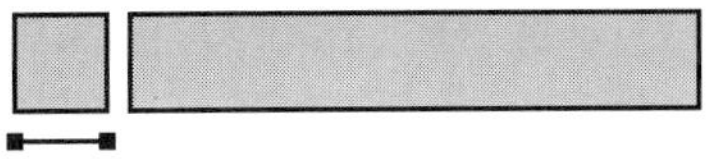

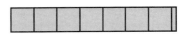

Cut square.

Continue cutting
strip into squares.

finished
side

straight
grain

#S2-S14 RECTANGLES

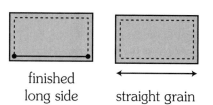

finished long side   straight grain

Note: "+" means add ¹⁄₁₆" to listed number.

Cut strip width.

Cut rectangle.

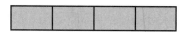

Continue cutting strip into rectangles this way.

#S2-S14 RECTANGLES

Size	Cutting	
fin. long side	cut strip width	cut rectangle
S2		
2"	1½"	2½"
2¾+	1⅞+	3¼+
3"	2"	3½"
4"	2½"	4½"
4¼"	2⅝"	4¾"
S3		
3"	1½"	3½"
4¼"	1⅞+	4¾"
4½"	2"	5"
6"	2½"	6½"
12"	4½"	12½"
S4		
4"	1½"	4½"
4¼"	1½+	4¾"
5"	1¾"	5½"
6"	2"	6½"
8"	2½"	8½"
S5		
5"	1½"	5½"
S6		
6"	1½"	6½"
S7		
7"	1½"	7½"
S8		
8"	1½"	8½"
S9		
9"	1½"	9½"
S10		
10"	1½"	10½"
S12		
12"	1½"	12½"
S13		
6"	4½"	6½"
S14		
4¼"	2"	4¾"

#T1 TRIANGLES

Size	Cutting		
fin. short side	cut strip width	cut square	cut in half diagonally to make two triangles
¾"	1⅝"	1⅝"	
⅞"	1¾"	1¾"	
1"	1⅞"	1⅞"	
1+	1⅞+	1⅞+	
1¼"	2⅛"	2⅛"	
1⅜+	2¼"	2¼"	
1½"	2⅜"	2⅜"	
1¾"	2⅝"	2⅝"	
2"	2⅞"	2⅞"	
2⅛"	3"	3"	
2½"	3⅜"	3⅜"	
3"	3⅞"	3⅞"	
3¼"	4⅛"	4⅛"	
3½"	4⅜"	4⅜"	
3⅝"	4½"	4½"	
3⅞"	4¾"	4¾"	
4"	4⅞"	4⅞"	
4¼"	5⅛"	5⅛"	
4½"	5⅜"	5⅜"	
6"	6⅞"	6⅞"	
7¼"	8⅛"	8⅛"	
8½"	9⅜"	9⅜"	

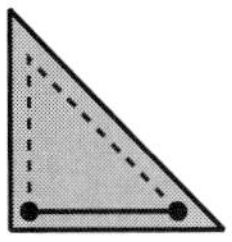

finished short side

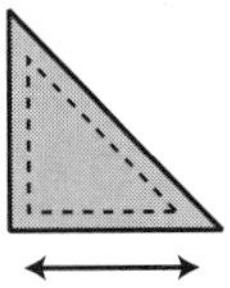

straight grain

#T1 2-PER-SQUARE TRIANGLES

Note: "+" means add ¹⁄₁₆" to listed number.

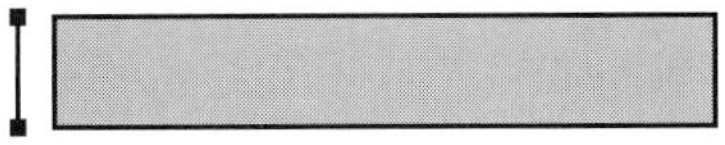

Cut strip width.

Cut square.

Cut square in half diagonally.

Continue cutting this way.

#T4 4-PER-SQUARE TRIANGLES

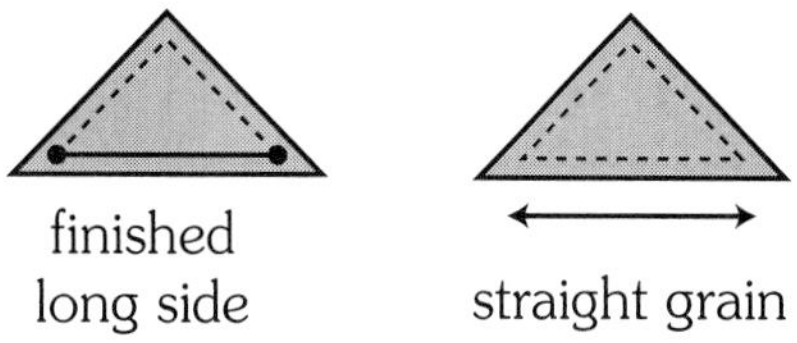

finished long side   straight grain

> **Note:** "+" means add ¹⁄₁₆" to listed number.

Cut strip width.

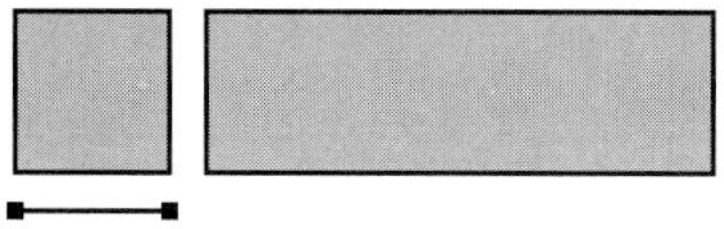

Cut square.

 Cut square in half along both diagonals.

Continue cutting this way.

#T8 45° HALF-DIAMOND TRIANGLES

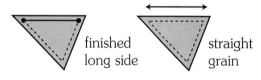

finished long side   straight grain

Cut strip width.

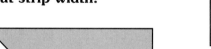

Cut off end at 45° angle.

Measure the listed distance from the angled end and cut diamond.

 Cut diamond in half diagonally.

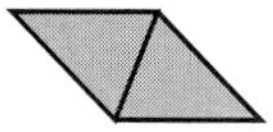

> **Note:** "+" means add ¹⁄₁₆" to listed number.

Continue cutting this way.

#T4 TRIANGLES

Size	Cutting		
fin. long side	cut strip width	cut square	cut square along both diagonals to make four triangles
1¼"	2½"	2½"	
1½"	2¾"	2¾"	
1¾"	3"	3"	
2"	3¼"	3¼"	
2⅛"	3⅜"	3⅜"	
2½"	3¾"	3¾"	
2½+	3¾+	3¾+	
2¾+	4+	4+	
3"	4¼"	4¼"	
3¼"	4½"	4½"	
3½"	4¾"	4¾"	
4"	5¼"	5¼"	
4¼"	5½"	5½"	
5"	6¼"	6¼"	
5⅛"	6⅜"	6⅜"	
6"	7¼"	7¼"	
7¼"	8½"	8½"	
8"	9¼"	9¼"	
8½"	9¾"	9¾"	
9"	10¼"	10¼"	
12"	13¼"	13¼"	
13¼"	14½"	14½"	

#T8 TRIANGLES

Size	Cutting			
fin. long side	cut strip width	cut angle 45°	cut diamond	cut in half diagonally
1¼"	1½+		1½+	
1½"	1¾"		1¾"	
1¾"	1⅞+		1⅞+	
2"	2⅛"		2⅛"	
2⅛"	2⅛+		2⅛+	
2¼+	2¼+		2¼+	
3"	2¾+		2¾+	
4¼"	3⅝+		3⅝+	
6"	4⅞+		4⅞+	

#T9 TRIANGLES

Size	Cutting			
fin. long side	cut strip width	cut angle 45°	cut parallelogram	cut in half diagonally
2⅛"	1⅛+		2¾+	
2¼+	1¼"		2⅞+	
2½"	1¼+		3+	
3"	1⅜+		3⅜+	
4¼"	1¾+		4¼+	
5½+	2⅛+		5¼"	
6"	2¼+		5½+	
8½"	3+		7¼+	
10⅝"	3⅝+		8¾+	

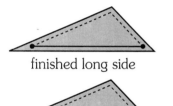

finished long side

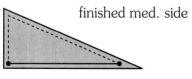

straight grain

Note: "+" means add ¹⁄₁₆" to listed number.

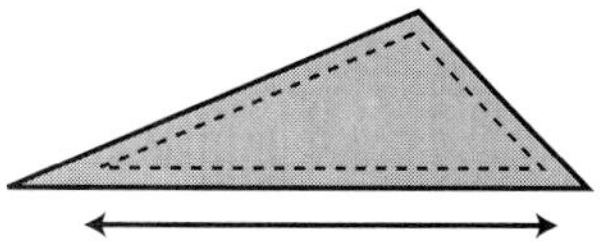

#T9 45°-22½°-112½° TRIANGLES

Cut strip width.

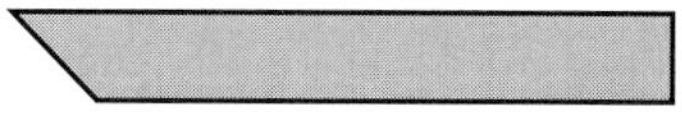

Trim end at a 45° angle.

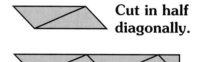

Subcut parallel to angled end.

Cut in half diagonally.

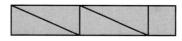

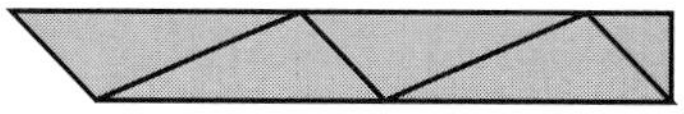

Continue cutting this way.

#T10 TRIANGLES

Size	Cutting		
fin. med. side	cut strip width	cut rectangle	cut in half diagonally
2⅛"	1½"	3⅝"	
3"	1⅞"	4½"	
3¼"	2"	4¾"	
4¼"	2⅜"	5¾"	
6"	3⅛"	7½"	

finished med. side

straight grain

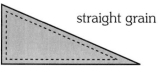

#T10 22½°-67½°-90° TRIANGLES

Cut strip width.

Subcut a rectangle.

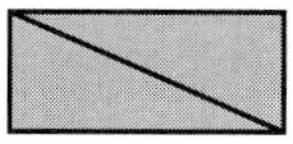

Cut in half diagonally to make 2 triangles.

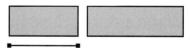

Continue cutting this way.

#T13 HALF-RECTANGLE TRIANGLES

Cut strip width listed.

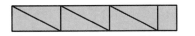

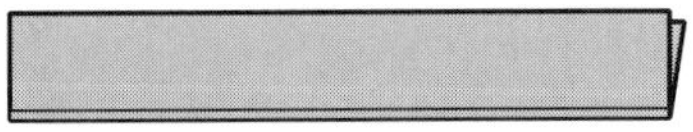

Fold strip in half and trim ⅛" from fold.

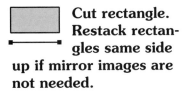 **Cut rectangle. Restack rectangles same side up if mirror images are not needed.**

 Cut in ½ diagonally.

Continue cutting this way.

Note: "+" means add ¹⁄₁₆" to listed number.

#T13 TRIANGLES

Size	Cutting			
fin. med. side	cut dbl. strip width	fold & trim ⅛"	cut rec- tangle	cut in ½ diagonally
2"	3½+		3¼+	
3"	4½+		4¼+	
4"	5½+		5¼+	

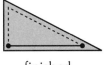

finished
med. side

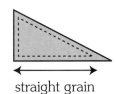

straight grain

#T14 TRIANGLES OF EQUAL HT. & WIDTH

Cut strip width.

Cut off end at a 2:1 angle*.

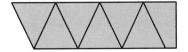

Subcut a parallelogram.

 Cut in half diagonally into 2 triangles.

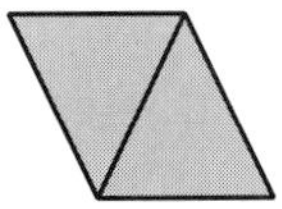

Continue cutting this way.

Note: "+" means add ¹⁄₁₆" to listed number.

#T14 TRIANGLES

Size	Cutting			
fin. short side	cut strip width	cut angle*	cut paral- lelo- gram	cut diagonally
2"	2¾+		2½"	
3"	3¾+		3⅜+	

finished
short side

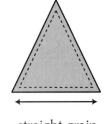

straight grain

*Make a guide for cutting the 2:1 angle for the T14 triangle as follows: Trace the T14 template on page 141. It doesn't matter whether or not you include seam allowances or what size pattern you trace; only the angle is needed. Tape the tracing to the unprinted side of your rotary ruler with the long side of the patch along the edge of the ruler.

#Z1 DIAGONAL TRAPEZOIDS

Size	Cutting			
fin. short side	cut strip width	cut square	cut in ½ diagonally	cut dist. from side
1+	3"	3"		1¼"
1½"	3⅞"	3⅞"		1½+
2"	4⅞"	4⅞"		1⅞+

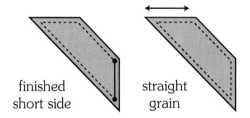

finished short side   straight grain

#Z1 DIAGONAL TRAPEZOIDS

Note: "+" means add ¹⁄₁₆" to listed number.

Cut strip width.

Cut square.

Cut in half diagonally. 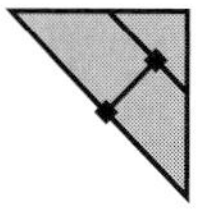   **Cut parallel to long side at distance listed.**

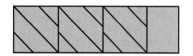

Continue cutting this way.

#Z3, Z10 & Z11 TRAPEZOIDS

Size	Cutting		
fin. long side	cut strip width	cut angle 45°	cut trapezoid length
Z3 6"	2½"		7¼"
Z10 6"	2¼"		7¼"
Z11 4"	1½"		5¼"

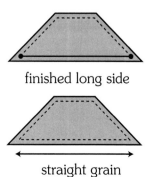

finished long side

straight grain

#Z3-Z11 TRAPEZOIDS

Cut strip width.

Cut angle 45°.

Position the listed measurement on the point and cut along the angled end of the Shapemaker 45 ruler to complete a trapezoid*.

Continue cutting this way.

*If you have only a regular ruler, you will need to cut a rectangle of the listed trapezoid length and cut off two corners at 45° angles in order to make a trapezoid.

HALF TRAPEZOIDS

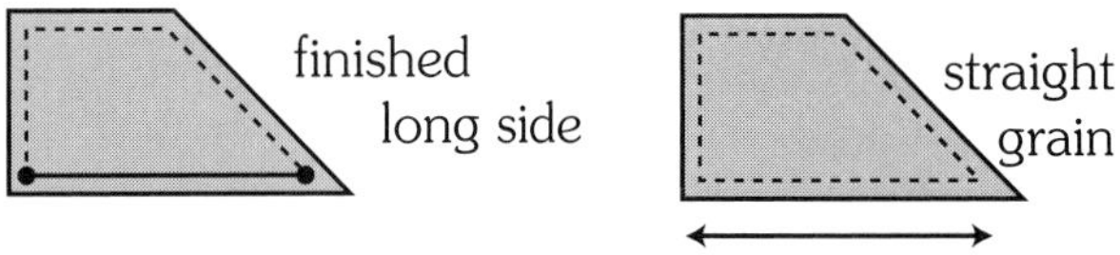

finished long side · straight grain

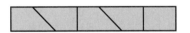

Cut strip width.

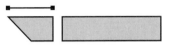

Use the S45 to subcut a half trapezoid*.

Use a regular ruler to sub- cut the next half trapezoid.

Continue cutting this way.

*If you have only a regular ruler, you may use the listed measurements to cut a rectangle, then cut off one corner at a 45° angle.

Note: "+" means add ¹⁄₁₆" to listed number.

#Z4, Z7 & Z9 HALF TRAPEZOIDS

Size	Cutting		
fin. long side	cut strip width	cut half trape- zoid	cut half trape- zoid
Z4			
3"	2"	3⅞"	3⅞"
4"	2½"	4⅞"	4⅞"
6"	3½"	6⅞"	6⅞"
Z7			
2⅛"	2"	3"	3"
3"	2⅝"	3⅞"	3⅞
Z9			
2⅛"	1⅛"	3"	3"
2½+	1¼"	3⅜+	3⅜+
3"	1⅜"	3⅞"	3⅞"
4¼"	1¾"	5⅛"	5⅛"
5⅛"	2"	6"	6"
6"	2¼"	6⅞"	6⅞"

DIAGONAL HALF TRAPEZOIDS

Cut strip width.

Cut off end at 45° angle.

Cut a parallelogram.

Cut in half diagonally. 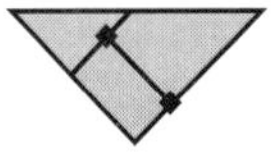 · **Parallel sub- cut as shown.**

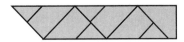

Continue cutting this way.

#Z6 DIAGONAL HALF TRAPEZOIDS

Size	Cutting				
fin. angled side	cut strip width	cut angle 45°	cut paral- lelo- gram	cut diagonally	cut dist. from side
2"	2⅝"		3⅝+		1⅞+

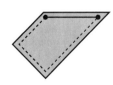 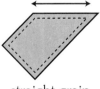

finished angled side · straight grain

Note: "+" means add ¹⁄₁₆" to listed number.

#Z8 22½° HALF TRAPEZOIDS

Size	Cutting	
fin. med. side	cut T9 triangle	cut parallel to triangle's med. side
3"	6"	1⅝"

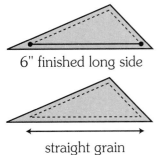

A. finished medium side   straight grain

#Z8 22½° HALF TRAPEZOIDS

Cut 6" 45°-22½°-112½° triangles as shown on the bottom half of this page.

Subcut the triangle parallel to the medium side.

Continue cutting this way.

#T9 TRIANGLES (6")

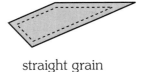

6" finished long side

straight grain

Note: "+" means add ¹⁄₁₆" to listed number.

#T9 45°-22½°-112½° TRIANGLES (6")

Cut 2¼+ strip width.

Trim end at a 45° angle.

Subcut parallel to angled end at distance of 5½+.

Cut in half diagonally.

Continue cutting this way.

The same name is
used for many
sizes. Find both
the pattern name
and size that you
need.

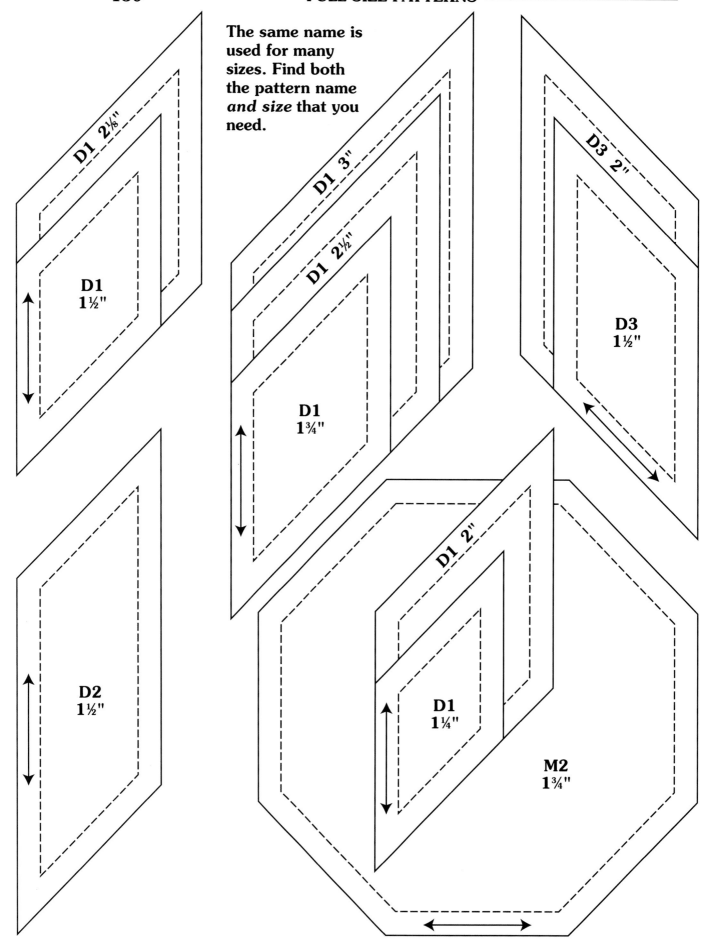

D1 2⅛"

D1
1½"

D1 3"

D1 2½"

D1
1¾"

D3 2"

D3
1½"

D2
1½"

D1 2"

D1
1¼"

M2
1¾"

The same name is used for many sizes. Find both the pattern name *and size* that you need.

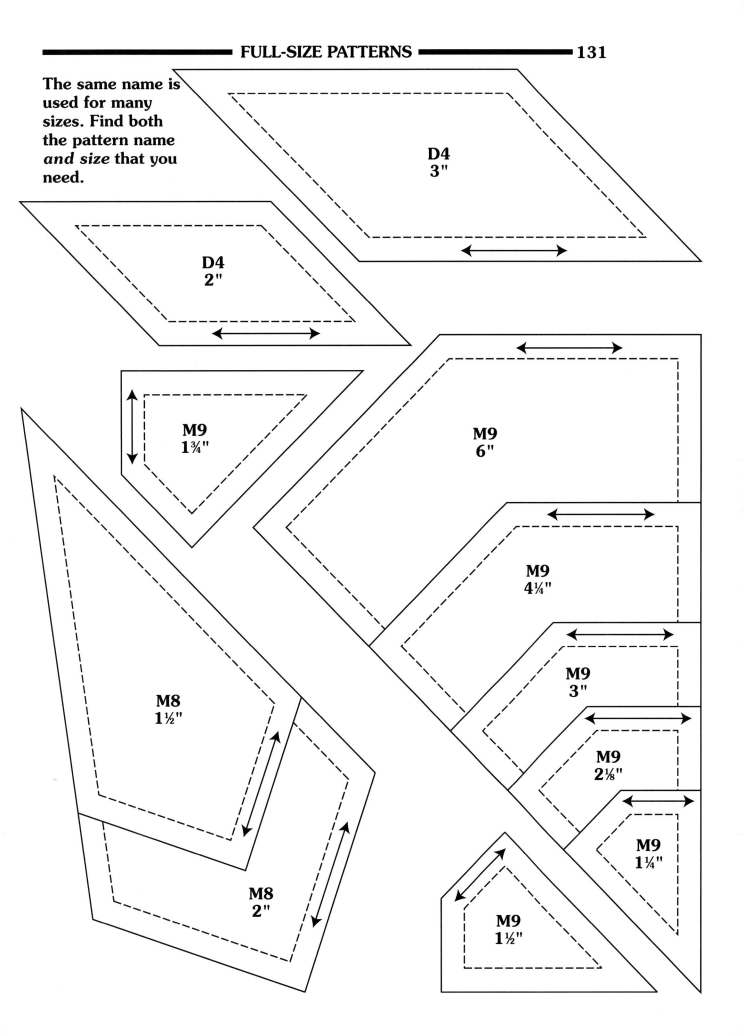

D4
3"

D4
2"

M9
1¾"

M9
6"

M9
4¼"

M9
3"

M9
2⅛"

M9
1¼"

M8
1½"

M8
2"

M9
1½"

The same name is
used for many
sizes. Find both
the pattern name
and size that you
need.

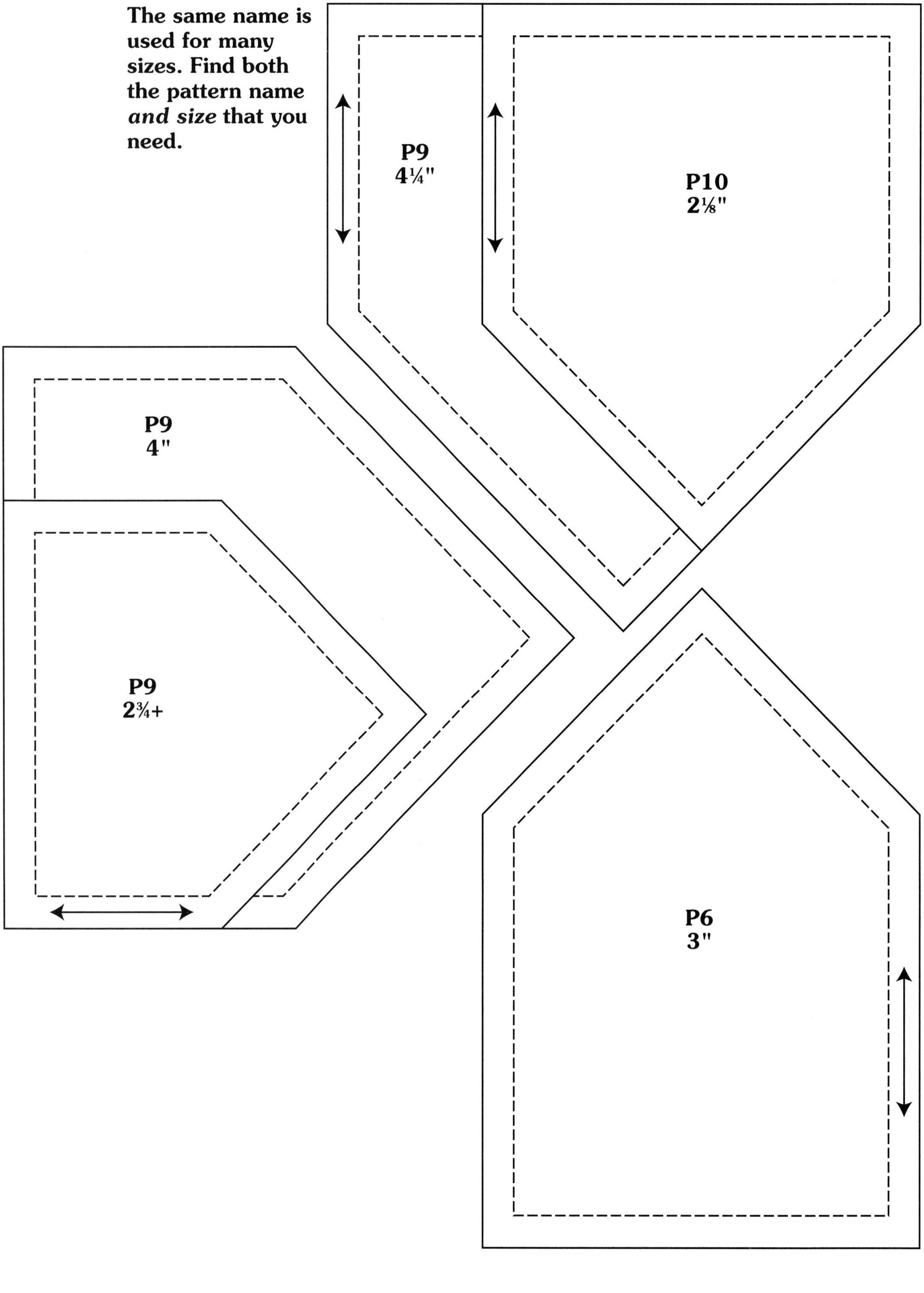

P9
4¼"

P10
2⅛"

P9
4"

P9
2¾+

P6
3"

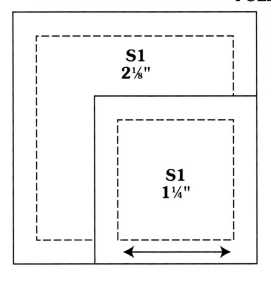

S1
2⅛"

S1
1¼"

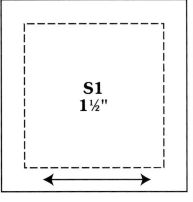

S1
1½"

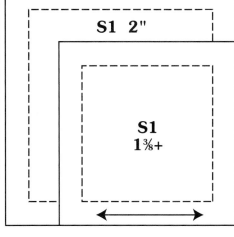

S1 2"

S1
1⅜+

The same name is used
for many sizes. Find
both the pattern name
and size that you need.

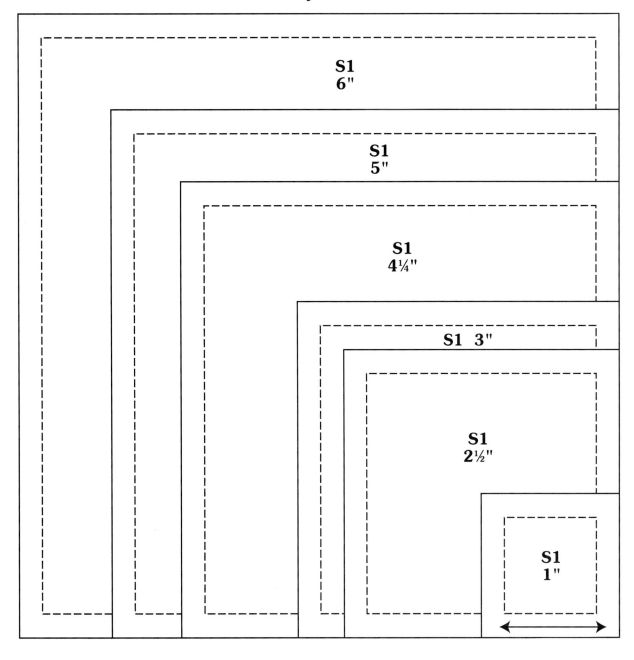

S1
6"

S1
5"

S1
4¼"

S1 3"

S1
2½"

S1
1"

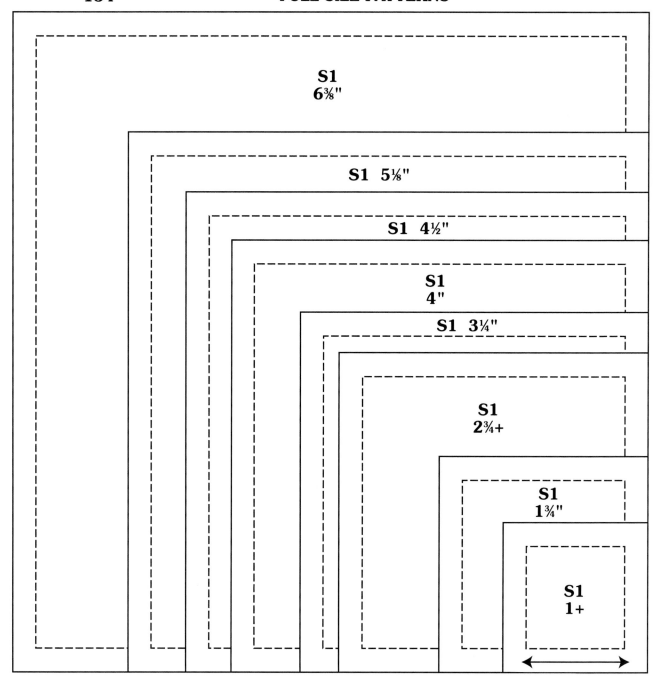

S1
6⅜"

S1 5⅛"

S1 4½"

S1
4"

S1 3¼"

S1
2¾+

S1
1¾"

S1
1+

The same name is used for many sizes. Find both the pattern name *and size* that you need.

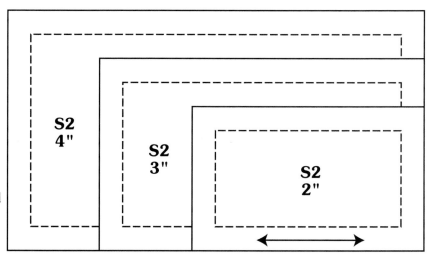

S2
4"

S2
3"

S2
2"

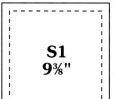

S1
9⅜"

Draw with finished sides 9⅜". Add seam allowances.

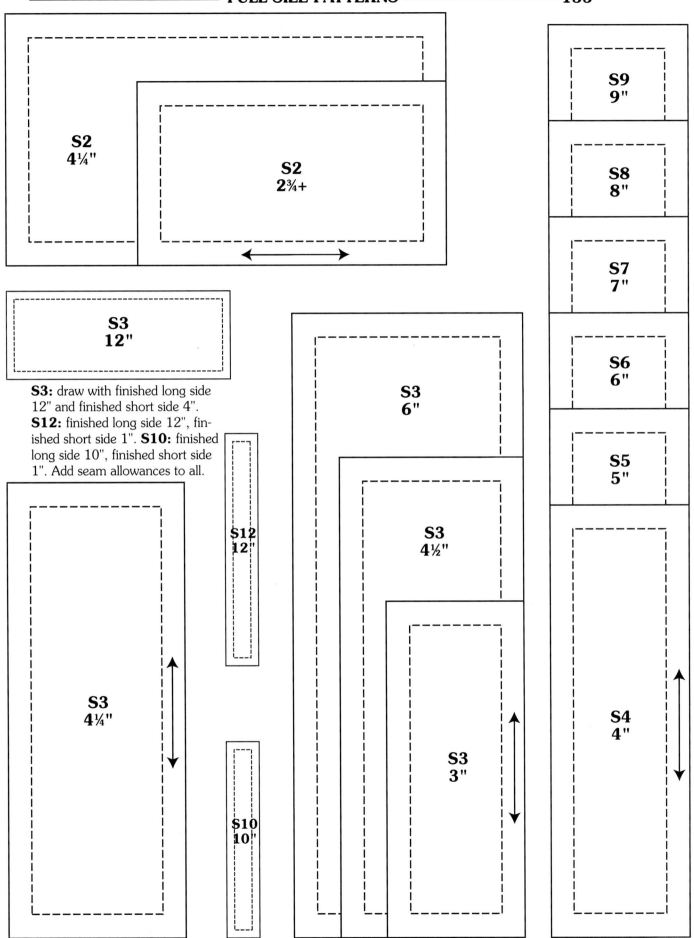

S2
4¼"

S2
2¾+

S9
9"

S8
8"

S7
7"

S6
6"

S5
5"

S3
12"

S3
6"

S3: draw with finished long side 12" and finished short side 4". **S12:** finished long side 12", finished short side 1". **S10:** finished long side 10", finished short side 1". Add seam allowances to all.

S12
12"

S3
4½"

S3
4¼"

S3
3"

S4
4"

S10
10"

The same name is used for many sizes. Find both the pattern name *and size* that you need.

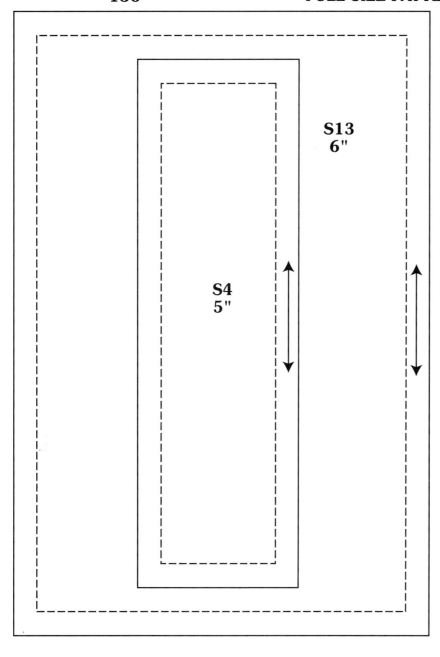

S13
6"

S4
5"

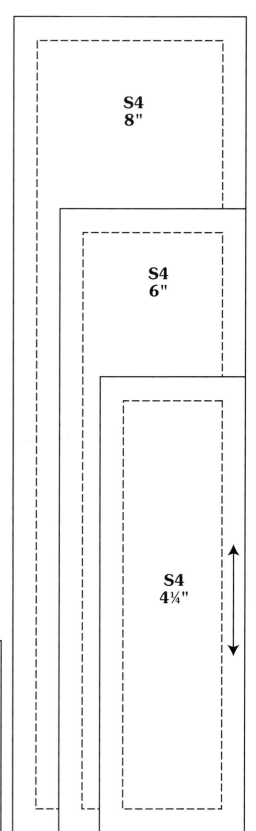

S4
8"

S4
6"

S4
4¼"

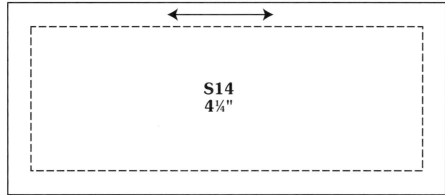

S14
4¼"

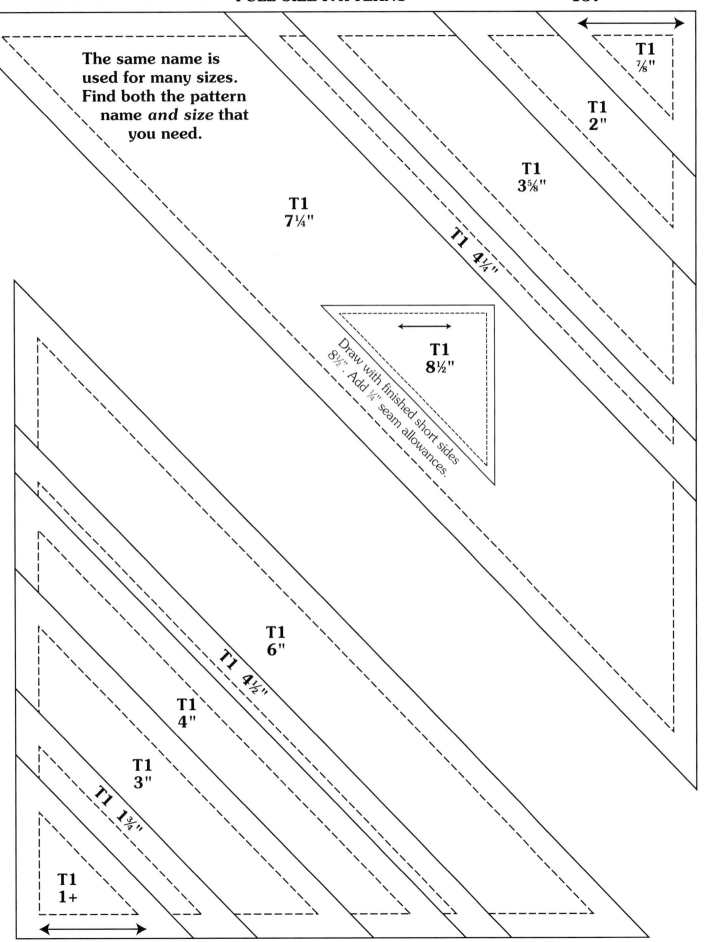

The same name is used for many sizes. Find both the pattern name *and size* that you need.

T1
⅞"

T1
2"

T1
3⅝"

T1
7¼"

T1 4¼"

T1
8½"

Draw with finished short sides 8½". Add ¼" seam allowances.

T1
6"

T1 4½"

T1
4"

T1
3"

T1 1¾"

T1
1+

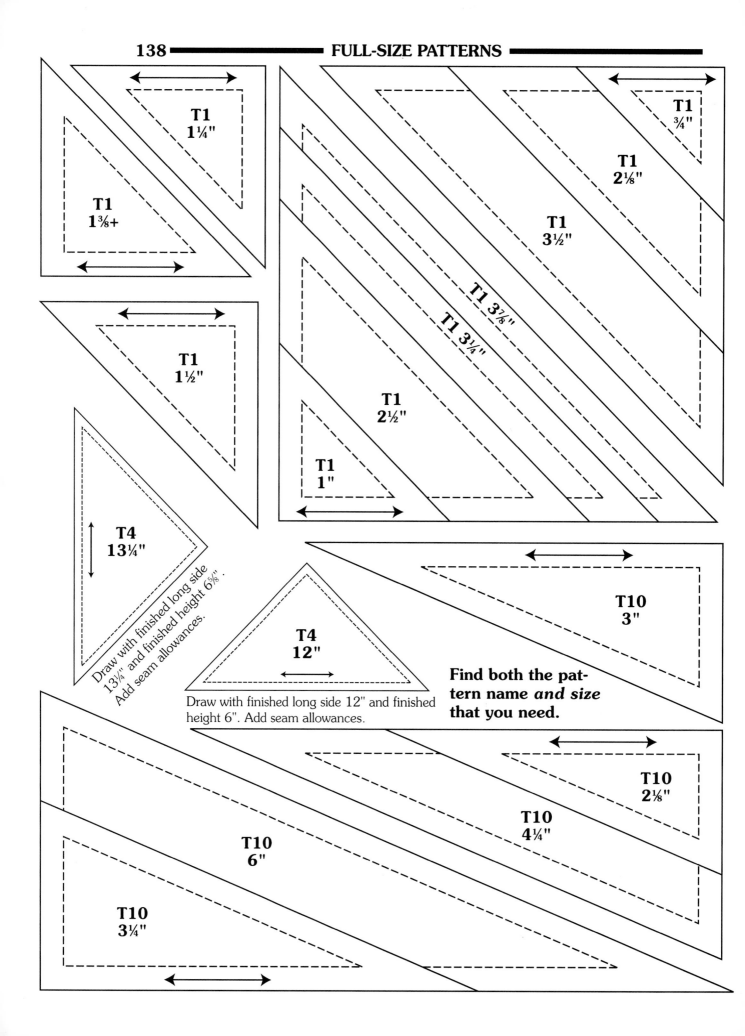

T1
1¼"

T1
1⅜+

T1
¾"

T1
2⅛"

T1
3½"

T1 3⅞"

T1 3¼"

T1
2½"

T1
1"

T1
1½"

T4
13¼"

Draw with finished long side 13¼" and finished height 6⅝". Add seam allowances.

T4
12"

Draw with finished long side 12" and finished height 6". Add seam allowances.

T10
3"

Find both the pattern name *and size* that you need.

T10
2⅛"

T10
4¼"

T10
6"

T10
3¼"

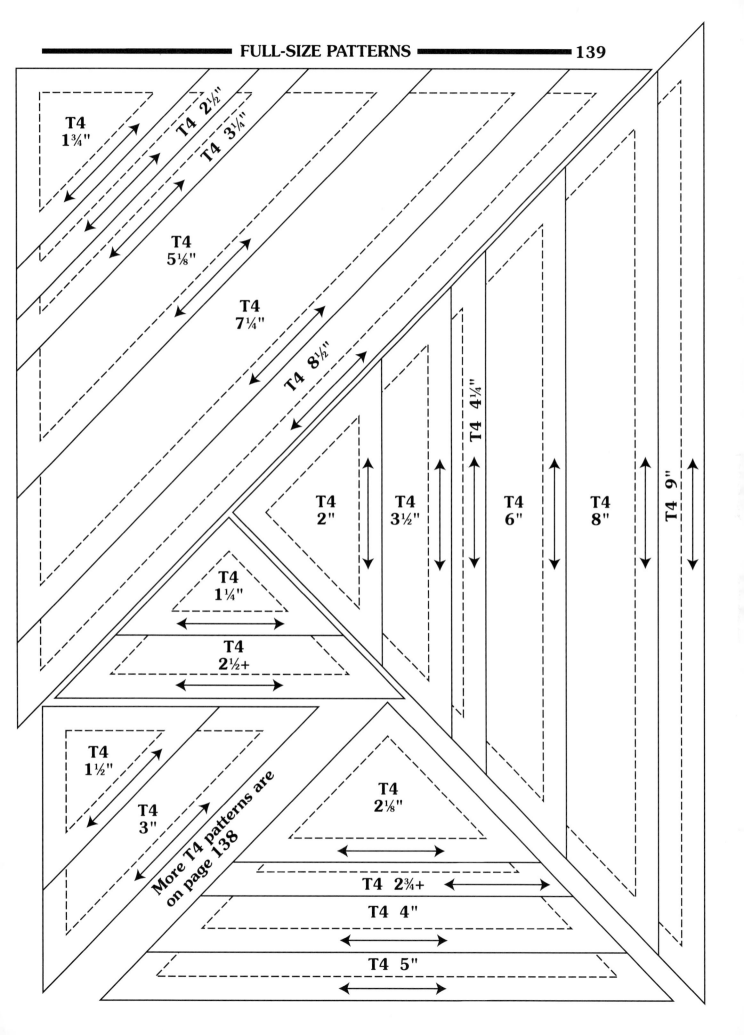

T4
1¾"

T4 2½"

T4 3¼"

T4
5⅛"

T4
7¼"

T4 8½"

T4 4¼"

T4 9"

T4
2"

T4
3½"

T4
6"

T4
8"

T4
1¼"

T4
2½+

T4
1½"

T4
3"

More T4 patterns are
on page 138

T4
2⅛"

T4 2¾+

T4 4"

T4 5"

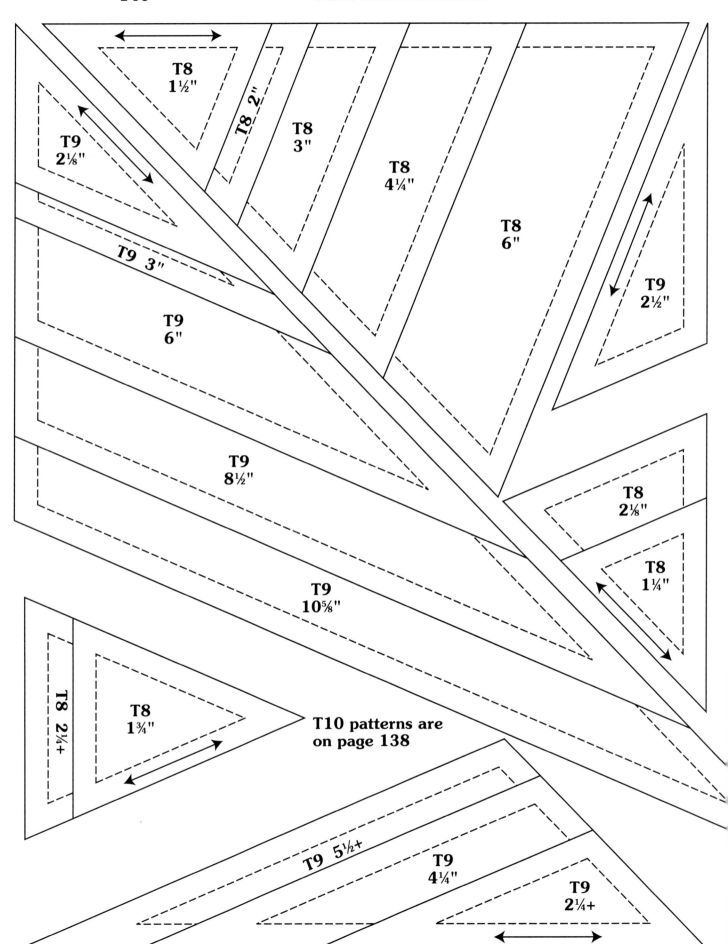

T8
1½"

T8 2"

T8
3"

T8
4¼"

T8
6"

T9
2⅛"

T9 3"

T9
6"

T9
2½"

T9
8½"

T8
2⅛"

T8
1¼"

T9
10⅝"

T8 2¼+

T8
1¾"

T10 patterns are
on page 138

T9 5½+

T9
4¼"

T9
2¼+

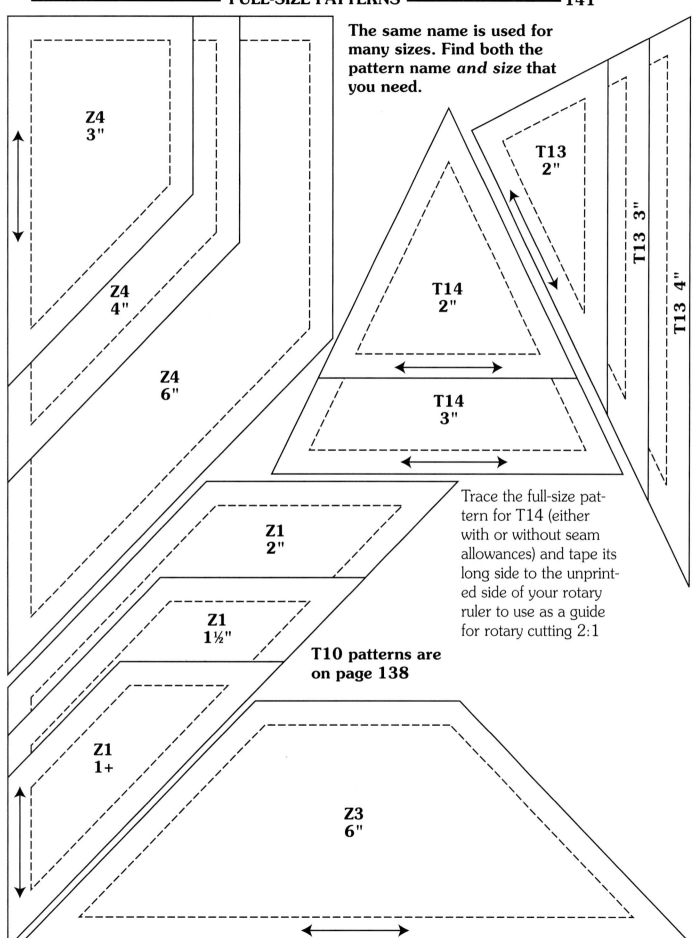

The same name is used for many sizes. Find both the pattern name *and size* that you need.

Z4
3"

Z4
4"

Z4
6"

T13
2"

T13 3"

T13 4"

T14
2"

T14
3"

Trace the full-size pattern for T14 (either with or without seam allowances) and tape its long side to the unprinted side of your rotary ruler to use as a guide for rotary cutting 2:1

Z1
2"

Z1
1½"

Z1
1+

T10 patterns are on page 138

Z3
6"

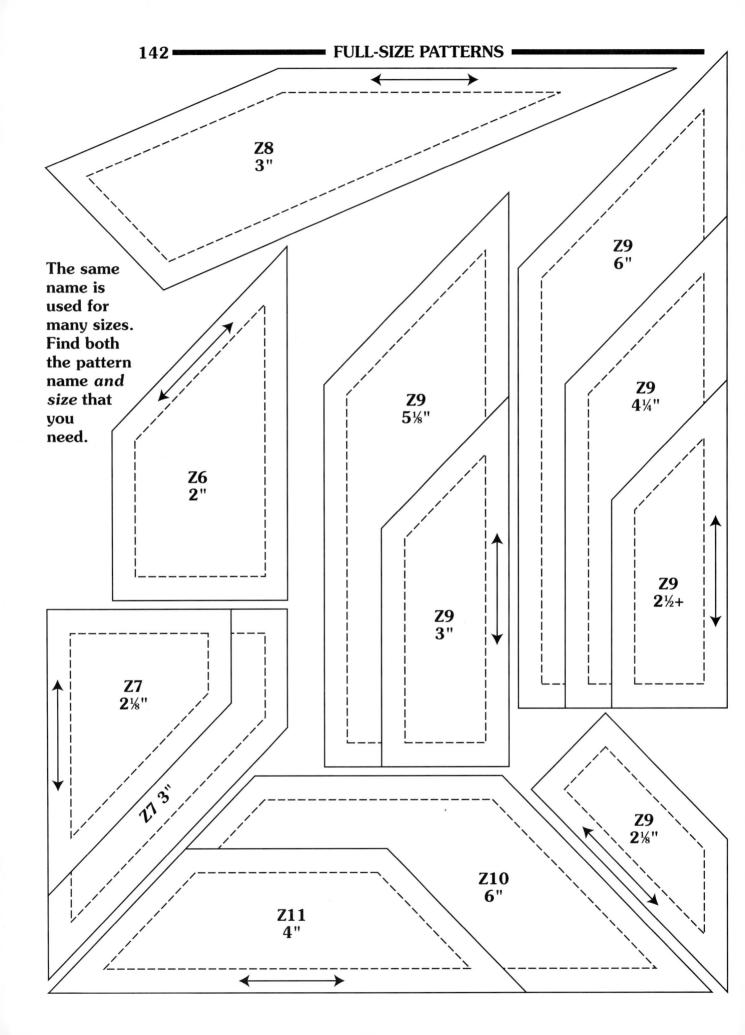

Z8
3"

The same
name is
used for
many sizes.
Find both
the pattern
name *and*
size that
you
need.

Z9
6"

Z9
4¼"

Z6
2"

Z9
5⅛"

Z9
3"

Z9
2½+

Z7
2⅛"

Z7 3"

Z9
2⅛"

Z10
6"

Z11
4"

Also available from Crosley-Griffith

QUILTING BOOKS

Judy Martin's Ultimate Rotary Cutting Reference

A must-have reference for every quilt-maker's library. Expert advice on rotary cutting plus charts telling yardage and dimensions for cutting 40 different shapes, including 9 kinds of triangles.

Pieced Borders: The Complete Resource

Judy Martin & Marsha McCloskey provide every detail of planning and constructing pieced borders. Twelve glorious quilt patterns and 200 border patterns are included.

Yes You Can! Make Stunning Quilts from Simple Patterns

Judy Martin's book of 14 appealing, yet easy, quilt patterns for rotary cutting.

JUDY MARTIN'S ULTIMATE ROTARY TOOLS

Point Trimmer

Reduce bulk in seams, avoid show-through, and align your patches perfectly for machine piecing by pretrimming seam allowances at points with this indispensable tool.

Shapemaker 45

Say "hello" to a wealth of new pattern possibilities. The S45 offers a better, faster way to rotary cut a multitude of patch shapes in countless sizes.

Shapemaker 45 Ready Reference Card

Indispensable charts tell strip and patch dimensions, with seam allowances included, for 6 shapes in all your favorite sizes. Step-by-step illustrations make it easy to master shapes with the S45.

Rotaruler 16

This is the premium rotary cutting ruler. Fine dashed lines make it easy to follow, and bold, clear numbers let you work faster. Precise rulings, including $\frac{1}{16}$" lines, mean more accuracy.

Sizemaster 90

Your ordinary ruler cuts only half the popular sizes commonly found in patchwork. This revolutionary ruler cuts your favorite shapes in the other half of the sizes.

Sizemaster 90 Ready Reference Card

Handy charts tell strip and patch dimensions, with seam allowances included, for 6 shapes in many useful sizes. Step-by-step illustrations make it easy to master your Sizemaster 90!

JUDY MARTIN'S ULTIMATE QUILT PATTERNS

Complete patterns in handy booklet form, with yardage and directions for quilts in four sizes. Even the quilting motifs are included. With these patterns, you can teach yourself to use Judy Martin's Ultimate Rotary Tools.

Judy's Fancy

An intriguing arrangement of handsome star blocks with a pieced border of smaller stars. Impressive!

Grandma's Porch

A striking new star block set in a Garden Maze set with a pieced Ribbon border.

Ask for these products at your favorite quilt retailer or write to Crosley-Griffith, P.O. Box 512, Grinnell, IA 50112 for a catalogue or to place an order. If you prefer, call us at our toll-free number, 1-800-642-5615 or visit our website at http://quilt.com/judym. Availability is subject to change.